Readings About Adolescent Literature

by

Dennis Thomison

The Scarecrow Press, Inc.
Metuchen, N.J.   1970

Copyright 1970, by Dennis Thomison
SBN 8108-0282-1

Table of Contents

Introduction

Part One. The Adolescent and His Reading 7
    The Role of Literature for Young People 7
        Edwin H. Cady
    For Everything There Is a Season 16
        G. Robert Carlsen
    A Time and Season for the Better Reader 26
        Margaret Edwards
    Promoting Adolescent Growth Through Reading 35
        Geneva R. Hanna
    Needed: More Literature Reading 41
        Hazel C. Hart

Part Two. Fiction for the Adolescent 45
    The Novel in the High School 45
        Lois Blau
    To Sail Beyond the Sunset 49
        G. Robert Carlsen
    The Adolescent in American Fiction 59
        Frederic I. Carpenter
    How Do I Love Thee? 69
        Margaret A. Edwards

Part Three. Non-fiction for the Adolescent 79
    Biographies for Teen-Agers 79
        Learned T. Bulman
    Finding the Right Poem 90
        Mary V. Lamson
    Astronomy Books for Children 99
        Donald and Elizabeth Macrae
    Books About Negroes for Children 110
        Charlemae Rollins

Part Four. Problems in Adolescent Literature 115
    Introduction
    Censorship and the Values of Fiction 117
        W. C. Booth
    Censorship and High School Libraries 133
        Richard G. Gannon
    Two Kinds of Censorship 136
        Hoke Norris
    Let 'Em Read Trash 139
        Robert G. Mood
    The Glitter and the Gold 150
        Richard S. Alm
    The Novel for the Adolescent 162
        Dwight L. Burton

Let the Lower Lights Be Burning	172
Margaret A. Edwards	
Literature for Adolescents--Pap or Protein?	186
Frank G. Jennings	
The Teenage Novel: A Critique	195
Vivian J. MacQuown	
Why Not the Bobbsey Twins?	199
Margaret Beckman	
Comic Books: A Teacher's Analysis	204
Dwight L. Burton	
Part Five. Giving A Book Talk	211
Book Talks	211
Amelia H. Munson	
Index	216

Introduction

What is "Literature for Adolescents"?

The recognition that the period of adolescence merits special attention is fairly recent, and certainly general acceptance of the concept of a separate literature for adolescents has come within the last forty years. Indeed, there are many people who still do not accept the idea. But for others, there is no doubt that adolescence like childhood is a special period requiring books written especially for that age.

The literature of the field can be divided into three basic types. First, there are many books which were written primarily for children but are sufficiently mature and have high enough interest levels to be satisfactory for the adolescent. For example, <u>Onion John</u>, a recent Newbery Award winner, is acceptable for the younger adolescent although written for children. Secondly, there is a newer area--those books which have been written primarily for the adolescent, of which <u>Seventeenth Summer</u> is a fine example. Finally, there are the adult books which are both interesting and readable, and therefore acceptable to young people. This group, of course, is the oldest within adolescent literature, for young people have always seemed to adopt some books which were popular with adults. <u>Robinson Crusoe</u> was originally written for adults but has long since been taken over as part of the literature for adolescents.

The Scope.

In general, "adolescence" has been defined in this book as the period from the seventh to the twelfth grade. This arbitrary division seemed necessary and justified, even while realizing that in most individuals the period or age begins earlier and ends later. For the most part, then, the readings are meant for the person planning to become a librarian in the junior or senior high school.

There has been no attempt to cover all areas taught in the

typical course covering Literature for Adolescents. For example, there are no articles on reading interests or adolescent psychology, but there is a reading on how to give book talks.

The Purpose.

There is in adolescent literature, more than in any other area of library science, the problem of suitable and sufficient text material. It is with this fact in mind that Readings About Adolescent Literature was planned--to supplement text material by providing meaningful articles from outstanding authors on a variety of subjects. Surely the basic reason for compiling a book of this nature is to help to provide an informational foundation about the field. But it is hoped that the articles will also provide a stimulus to further and wider reading through the discussion of outstanding books available for young people.

Acknowledgment.

I wish to thank the many editors, publishers, and authors who kindly gave me permission to include their articles in this book.

> Dennis Thomison
> Graduate School of Library Science
> University of Southern California
> Los Angeles, California

Part One. The Adolescent and His Reading

"The Role of Literature for Young People Today" by Edwin H. Cady. English Journal, 64:275-280, May, 1955. Reprinted with the permission of the National Council of Teachers of English.

On this question of the good literature can do for your young people--or the general question of what literature is good for--we who teach literature seem often to be a little confused and therefore (unnecessarily, I think) evasive--or even sometimes negative--with ourselves, our pupils, and the public. Because I am convinced that there is a reasonable ground for strong faith in ourselves and our cause, I would like to begin the discussion of the topic by suggesting to you--I almost said recalling with you--a brief and elementary theory of literature. I would like to start with a few things everybody knows.

First, that one can make a useful distinction between experience and events. Events may be said to happen objectively, externally to us; experience occurs subjectively, within the mind. It is related to events, but it is not the simple product of them. Experience may be said to be what the mind does with events, or does because of events, or makes out of events. In pointing this out to my students, I often use an illustration which has here, at least, a seasonal relevance. Saturday before last Syracuse played its "big," "traditional" football game against Colgate. The game is one of those magnificently irrational symbolic events which so often convulse American life (for the sake particularly of my friend the football coach, I am happy to be able to say that Syracuse won it this year). But, as I say to the students, suppose you were sitting in the stadium next to a friend from Colgate and you both saw a Syracuse half-back break away and run forty yards for a touchdown. The objective event would have been the same for both of you, but your experiences would be very different, in a sense opposite. The illustration is perhaps a crude one, but it helps to enforce the point: our experience is inward, and it is what the mind makes it to be.

A second point, which is also illustrated above, is that there is an important relationship between the kind of preparation the mind has for experience and the kind of experience it creates. Another illustration of this point is provided by the story, sometimes told of Andrew Dixon White, the first president of Cornell, to the effect that he once forbade a Cornell team to go to Philadelphia for what is now the great traditional Thanksgiving Day game with Penn. He could see no reason, the prexy is reported to have said, for transporting twenty-five young men and scholars all the way to Philadelphia to spend a couple of hours agitating a bag of wind about a pasture. That also helps suggest my third point, which is that an active power of the mind, a something we have long called Imagination, is perhaps the key factor in determining the quality, the strength, and the satisfactoriness of our experience. We must come out to meet events, not receive them passively, and the most interesting lives are those led by the persons with the best imaginations. And so (fourth and last), experience, in the sense of the word we have been using here, is the most important part of an individual's life. In a meaningful sense, it IS his life, the all-important part to which his biological being is merely a servant.

Still on a most elementary level, if one looks at the extremely valuable aids to understanding ourselves made available by the anthropologists and other "culturologists" of our time, he sees that there are no people so primitive that their culture does not contain some form of the arts. One might say that being human means, among other things, being artistic. And if one asked himself the reason why this should be so, he might find answers partly in the all-importance of "experience" as outlined above, and partly in one of the several definitions of art. For it is possible to define art, and the arts, as being the modes by which a superior imagination, functioning at the top of its powers, can express itself in a form, a form which, in turn, can communicate to us by stimulating and affecting, by commanding, our imaginations. By commanding our imaginations, the arts force them, so to speak, to create for us experience more vivid, more intense, and more satisfactorily shaped than any experience we can ordinarily (or perhaps ever) create for ourselves alone.

Now literature is art; it is the art which works in the medium of words and employs them to command our imaginations to create this better, this esthetic experience for us. It is perhaps purest when it is most purely verbal, as in certain kinds of poetry. But literature seems, at least to us who are very much concerned with it, to be more widely powerful than some other kinds of art, precisely because it deals with words. Words are so basic to so many functions of the mind that it is difficult, ordinarily impossible, to keep literature "pure." Its implications bulge out through the net of pure verbal magic. Literature becomes involved with ideas of all sorts, with political and social institutions, and with every variety of the everyday forms of individual human action and emotion which we often think of as "dramatic." Thus literature becomes involved, not only with much if not all of human life, at least in our culture, but also with many of the other arts, often hybridizing with them in such forms as song, the drama, opera, and others. Even as apologists for literature, we need feel no embarrassment in pointing to its esthetic power and to the deeply intimate appeal to men's minds of literature's medium--words--especially when endowed with esthetic power. It is certainly not without significance, to choose only the most telling example, that at the heart of each of the great world religions there is a book, a Scripture, literature put at the service of religion.

All of these things being true (and certainly there is nothing startlingly new about them), it becomes fairly easy to say what literature is good for: or, what is most to our purpose here, to say what literature can do for the young people who are our pupils. Before literature can do anything at all, of course, it must be read. And it is our function and our privilege as teachers to help young people learn to read literature. Not just learn to read (pace our invaluable remedial-reading colleagues), not just learn to cover so many words with so many eyesweeps in so many seconds with such-and-such an ability to grasp and recall factual data referred to by the words. But learn to read literature, to "get" it, as we all say, to have the engrossing, well-formed experiences which it is the artistic function of literature to help us to have. By teaching the pupil to "get" literature, in that sense, we can help him to open very important doors to the good life--and that is what literature is most of all good for.

The first door literature can help the student to open for himself is the door to a richer and more satisfying emotional and imaginative life. That is one of the most important doors in life. Upon whether it is properly opened or not may hang the question of whether or not the individual pupil ever achieves a stable and satisfying psychic life.

A hundred years ago Henry David Thoreau observed that the great majority of men were living lives of quiet desperation rather than the life of natural joy and transcendental illumination which he thought they ought to be leading. Leaving Thoreau's special ideas out of the question, I think it probable that the majority of men in all times have led lives of something like desperation, more or less quietly, and I think also that there can be no doubt at all that Thoreau's diagnosis would be found true of the great majority of people in our own time, except that nowadays our desperation is less and less quiet. And I submit to you that perhaps in all times, one reason for quiet, personal desperation is the intolerableness of the dim, gray, undifferentiated nature of much if not all of our daily experience. Most of our habitual daily activities have lost their power to stimulate our imaginations, and even new events more often merely frighten or disorganize us than help us create significant experience. Now it is obviously, I think, one of the great functions of any culture, and most especially of the artistic side of any culture, to allay our quiet desperation by giving us the opportunity to create vivid, well-organized, and satisfying experience. One of the measures of the success of a culture is, of course, the degree to which it affords such opportunities to the people who are loyal to it.

It will be no news to anybody that our own culture has been and still is passing through a time of troubles in this as in other ways. The massive demands for personal and social readjustments brought into being by the urbanization and the industrialization of our

The Adolescent and His Reading

culture have thus far been only partially answered. Consequently, confusion and cultural erosion, sometimes very profound cultural erosion, have bedevilled many individuals and to a greater or lesser extent robbed them of their power to experience true esthetic and other cultural satisfactions. The result has been all the worst manifestations of our mass-entertainment industries. Vice and perversity, gambling, violence, sentimentality, and brainless sensationalism--dozens of forms of vulgarity and self-destructiveness--wax rich and tyrannical everywhere (not just in America) in modern society. And they are able to do so because they fill, at least with something, the gray vacuum of our daily desperation.

Such is the world, sometimes the only kind of world, in which the parents of our pupils live and in which our pupils are growing up. That they need the best--along with the worst, which they will get from the mass entertainment industries anyway--our culture can give them is all too tragically obvious. And one of the ways in which they can get the best is through the arts, and especially literature: if we can teach them to really read it.

But as pupils, that is, as young people, they have needs, just as they have opportunities and hopes, which their elders have outgrown. Being young, our pupils, as you teachers know only too well, are barbarians. And they are barbarians in two ways: first by natural superstition; second, by innocence. Their barbarism by natural superstition has a physical basis. Since they are living in a period of intense physical vitality and euphoria, they naturally suppose that the physical life and its attendant modes of expression are a lasting basis for the good life. One could not completely disillusion them of this superstition if he would, and surely one ought not to try. Let them make the most of it while they can! The danger is that they will grow up confirmed in this superstition and then, deserted by euphoria and snap, awake some day to a bleak and empty adult world. This is what we can help to prevent.

The barbarism of our pupils' innocence is also natural, but it is of the very greatest immediate concern to us as teachers as it is also to all parents. All innocently, and ignorantly, children are naturally alienated from the society and culture in which they have to grow up. They understand even less about it than adults do, and they often find its customs, rituals, laws, rules, and patterns stupid and intolerable. They balk and rebel, conform only gradually, drag their feet as they are shoved or enticed from plateau to plateau of learning and acceptance. And it is precisely in this realm that literature, and the teaching of literature, can help to open two more important doors to the pupil. By accustoming him to move easily in the world of beliefs, ideas, words and other symbols, and ways of understanding things in general of his culture, literature can open the door to a young reader, the door to a keener perception of the world around him. It has been surmised that what made Benjamin Franklin the greatest man of his age was his simple clear-sightedness, his ability to see the world of nature and the world of men more plainly and objectively (but in tune with the major understandings of his era) than perhaps anyone else. Without some measure of this ability to harmonize with the culture of his time and place, to see as it sees, no one can be a useful or prosperous citizen. With it, he may be an eccentric, or even seriously neurotic, and still be a useful, or even an important, member of society.

And finally, not only can the right sort, and the right fullness, of literary experience help a pupil to a keener perception of the world around him; it may help open the door to something many Americans are intensely (and I think often misguidedly) concerned over--the door to "loyalty." A good deal of the bumbling talk about "loyalty," by both some of our elected, and some of our self-elected, representatives has shown that the bumblers are dimly aware that there is more to the question than the simple test: Is he loyal? Will he betray us? Even some of the most benighted of the over-simplifiers have sensed, however dimly, that when you have to ask that ultimate, shocking question, when you think you ought to require a gratuitous oath or try somehow to force the display of a badge of loyalty, something very precious and essential has been lost. If the history, to take just one of many available examples, of Italy under Fascism shows anything at all, it shows, and unmistakably, how poisonous to true loyalty that kind of outward show, that kind of parade and braggadocio about loyalty can be. For the essence of true loyalty is a full, and largely unconscious, participation in the life of one's country, in the life of one's culture. Loyalty is a form of love. It is like the love one has for his wife, or his best friend, or God--he may tell his wife, very carefully; he may show it, but probably not tell it to his friend; he may tell it to God, secretly in prayer: but in all four cases of love, he takes a very serious risk who would kiss and tell. He takes the risk of corrupting his love and becoming a hypocrite and a cynic. That is what happened to Mussolini--his divisions, some of whom later fought magnificently against the Nazis out of a quietly self-generated love for Italy, were beaten before they fought for Il Duce. Their loyalty to him had long since been worn away in parades and demonstrations; they fought and lost like cynics. To understand loyalty, one would do much better to read Josiah Royce than a list of Senators we could all fill out.

The culture we live in is not, after all, quite like the culture of a primitive people: it differs in certain important ways. Our culture, our "way of life," is so complex that observers are often tempted to call it ways of life. Ours is a culture of cultures, the heritage of an infinitely varied ancestry. Our culture has bewildering vertical ramifications of economic, educational, and social grouping, equally complicated horizontal differences from one regional, religious, linguistic, or racial group to another. It is not that these complications are insurmountable. It is our proud boast to the world that America is in this way, as in others, a new experiment in human living in which successful unity can be found in diversity without obliterating the diversity in the unity; and we are, thank God, making progress toward solving the problems this experiment presents us with. All hope of solving these problems rests on understanding from one group toward another and on widening understanding being communicated to our young people as they grow up to citizenship. Teaching of every kind can help, and has helped immensely, in creating those understandings. But the creators of literature--especially the creators of the American novel from the time when, in the generation of Mark Twain, William Dean Howells, Henry James, Edward Eggleston, and their disciples, the problems of American life first began to be seriously and systematically treated in fiction--the authors, have made notable contributions to our understanding. Anyone who thinks and communicates effectively makes patterned abstractions (of words, figures, or whatever it may be) and employs them to affect the imaginations of his audience. The artist has the advantage of being able to command the whole imagination, powerfully rousing the emotions, reaching down into some of the unconscious depths of the mind, for instance, in ways not often available to the statistician, the lawyer, or the social scientist. And the novelist particularly, with his unlimited range through human life, his broad scope in which to work, has advantages with this kind of material which are not shared by any other artist except, perhaps, the maker of movies--would you call him a cinematist? Almost anyone in this room could sit down and in half-an-hour make an impressive list of the American (or British, French, Spanish, Russian, German, and so forth and so on) novels which have profoundly shaped people's ways of imagining themselves, their countries and societies, and the roles which they ought to play with regard to those countries or societies. In making such book available to our pupils, available to them in the sense that they "get" the experiences to be had from the novels, we help open doors to new and deeper understandings. Making such full, such total or "whole" experiences and understandings available, we help them to fuller and truer participation in American life and so toward genuine loyalty. The man we have to fear most in American life is the bewildered and alienated bystander, the desperate seeker, the lost soul who does not "belong." We have nothing to fear, I believe, from the whole-hearted participator, no matter how varied or special, how many-minded his participation.

There are two things I have not spoken of today, though both are germane to what I have been saying. One of them is religion. I do not share the nineteenth century hope, born of the Victorian dilemma, that literature can somehow be made an effective substitute for God. I don't think it can. But I am neither commissioned to talk here about religion nor equipped with any expertness to talk about it if I had been so commissioned. I think literature can sometimes do some of the same things for people as religion. I think literature can do, as I have tried to be careful to say, <u>help</u> to do the things I have claimed for it today. But I also think that literature and religion have their places working side by side in people's lives, not in opposition, not one substituting for the other.

The other thing I have hardly mentioned is specific literature, what novels, poems, plays, essays we should turn to for the good that is in literature. That failure (if it is one) has also been deliberate. One friend urged on me, somewhat cynically, I thought, the advice that I must be very concrete about this. "They want you to prepare some classes for them, so they won't have to do the work," he said. But I didn't believe it. As teachers of literature you are quite as capable as I of selecting the stuff you want to teach. The only bit of professional pedagogical concern I have to urge is that we give a proper place to the teaching of literature as such in our curricular planning. If literature can have anything like the values I have been claiming for it, then the teaching of literature, in the sense I have been giving it, is one of the highest functions, if not the very highest function, of the teacher of English. I am certainly in no sense a professional in the field of English curricula, but as I have heard them discussed from time to time, I think I have never heard the serious teaching of literature for the sake of its greatest values discussed. Perhaps this is a frontier for curricular research and planning, though it may only be my ignorance that makes it seem so.

At any rate, as teachers of literature I bid you good cheer. There is the greatest and the most pressing need in your pupils and within the culture we must share with them, for the very best work we can do. And this remains true whether or not our pupils, their parents, and much of the general American community realize it only very dimly, or even realize it not at all.

"For Everything There Is a Season" by G. Robert Carlsen. Top of the News, 21:103-110, January 1965. Reprinted with the permission of the American Library Association.

"For everything there is a season, and a time for everything under heaven."

When my daughter was about fifteen, she came home one evening and precipitated a family crisis. She had been asked to her first formal dance. After the excitement of the invitation had worn off, we got to the crux of the matter: "I haven't got a thing I can wear."

Being frugal people, we suggested that perhaps with a brooch or a scarf she could dress up one of her Sunday school dresses. But when she and her mother looked through her closet, it was apparent that these dresses were too little-girlish for such a momentous occasion. Next we suggested that perhaps she could wear one of her mother's dresses. Faculty wives have two old formals, one about three years old and the other about ten, that they alternate in wearing on the few occasions that call for them. When my daughter tried them on, she looked at herself in the mirror and broke down crying. So reluctantly we gave in. She would have to have a new dress. It consisted of yards and yards of pink nylon net gathered at the waist. She was delighted. But she asked her mother to try it on and when she saw it on my wife, she was once again reduced to tears by the ludicrous spectacle my wife made in a dress designed for a fifteen-year-old.

"For everything there is a season, and a time for everything under heaven."

This morning we are talking about the season of young adult's reading--about the later part of the period we label adolescence. My remarks are confined to the reading of young adults aged sixteen to twenty, that period when young people are in the last two years of high school or the first two years of college. Of course, anyone who has worked with young people realizes that there are always exceptions to any statement that is made. However, we know a great deal about the reading habits and interests of this group. This information applies to perhaps 95 per cent of young readers in this age bracket. Strangely enough, we have failed in our reading guidance programs to make use of what we do know.

This information can be grouped into the following five areas:

1. We know that the traditional reading programs of the secondary schools are failing miserably in developing any enthusiasm about reading. For several years, I have been collecting "reading autobiographies" from adults. Most of my accounts come from people who ultimately became "reading adults." Therefore, they probably present the most favorable possible picture of what happens in the process of growing up with books. From the five hundred cases, these are typical samples:

The most detestable literary experience I had was in Junior year English. We spent three long weary months studying Macbeth which was followed by three dull months also combing Paradise Lost in the same ridiculous manner. It was the most frightful example of lazy and uninspiring teaching I have ever seen.

* * *

Moving into high school also moved me into the classics. First in line was David Copperfield which I thoroughly detested and because of this book, I took a hearty dislike to Charles Dickens. Books you had to read were the worst kind.

* * *

I liked learning grammar and found it easy. But reading was a different matter. A class reading Julius Caesar, The Tempest, and As You Like It haltingly and without understanding can be a tedious business. It took many periods, too, it seems to me now. I shudder now at my introduction to Shakespeare. I remember seeing at the Old Vic Theater at the Chicago World's Fair, Twelfth Night, As You Like It, and The Taming of the Shrew and thinking with delighted amazement: "This is Shakespeare?"

* * *

When school started in the fall my English teacher handed out a required reading list. When she wouldn't let anyone make substitutions to the list, I immediately rebelled against reading anything other than just enough to get by.

* * *

In high school, my English teachers had taken as their province the ruining of any interest I had in reading. I am still bitter about their attitude that the proper aims of the English class were twofold: learning to diagram the hell out of any sentence, and showing how literature can only be properly understood if you memorized all the dates and names in the book. I can truthfully say that I was never challenged in any sense in any English class I had in high school.

* * *

English teachers who insisted on the memorization of parts of the "Ancient Mariner" or that I get the meaning of Shakespeare and Addison began to bore and irritate me to the point that I almost came to believe that the great works of literature were creations devised by authors for the sole purpose of torturing young students. Most of the fun and sense of wonder that I had felt for reading earlier deserted me.

* * *

In my Junior year I was introduced to Theodore Dreiser through <u>Sister Carrie</u> and from there delved into several other of the school of realists and naturalists. Here, getting a taste of hard life and hard sex, and naturally wanting more, I went to the trash.

The contentions of teachers that unless students stretch to reach something over their heads, they will not grow--that even though they don't appreciate it now, they will be glad they were exposed to it in the future, are cliches with little basis in fact. Our school programs generally teach students to spurn reading rather than lead them to seek it.

2. We know that the general pattern of growth in reading tastes during the adolescent period is through the following types of books:

First, young people find their satisfaction in the adolescent book: the book written especially for him, to evoke his emotions, problems, dreams, and life. These are books such as those written by John Tunis, Ann Emery, Mary Stolz, Adrien Stoutenberg, Margaret Maize Craig, James Kjelgaard, to mention only a few. These authors are producing works of some real merit from a literary point of view and adolescents have chosen them as among their favorite authors.

As the young person starts to grow beyond this stage, he will usually choose, first, the popular adult book. Ordinarily, this is the kind of work that is standardly on the best seller list. It has wide popular readership for a few years and then drops out of sight. Recently books like <u>Exodus</u>, <u>Mrs. Mike</u>, <u>Hawaii</u>, <u>Fail Safe</u> have been favorites with the young adults. Occasionally such books may remain favorites among the young adults for thirty or so years. <u>Gone with the Wind</u> has probably been kept alive largely by the adolescent reader.

The third step toward maturity is reached when the young reader starts to dip into the works of serious contemporary literature. These are the books that appear on college reading lists in courses centering on contemporary literature. They are the ones that critics feel make up the body of contemporary literature and may well live for several hundred years. At present, the more mature young adult is reading Camus, Golding, Salinger, Baldwin, as well as earlier writers of the twentieth century, such as Lewis, Maugham, Hemingway, and Wolfe.

The final step in growth in reading leads the reader to an interest in the classics: in Shakespeare and Sophocles, in Fielding and Austin, in Thackeray and Hardy. Ordinarily, this stage is not reached, save as it is forced on people, much before full maturity.

The young adult about whom we are talking, the young person between sixteen and twenty, is most usually reading in the two middle stages. He has passed beyond the reading of the adolescent book, but he is not yet ready for the classics of our literary heritage.

3. The young adult readers have literary idols. Each generation seems to select a handful of authors that speak to them directly as a group. Ordinarily, the college student finds the authors first, and quickly the more sophisticated high school students follow

the lead. To be "in the group" one must read and discuss certain books and authors. In the twenties, Millay and Lewis and Dreiser and Sinclair were such idols. In the thirties, Farrell and Wolfe, Dos Passos, and Hemingway had taken their place. It was already somewhat passe to admit that one read Millay or was moved by The Jungle. The idols of the forties (disrupted by war) tended to be Mailer and Eliot. In our own period, they are Baldwin and Salinger, Golding and Waugh, Updyke and Dylan Thomas. As we shall see a bit later, these writers have something in common. The basic tastes of the young adult seem not to have changed very much over the years, although the writers they read have.

4. The young adult chooses or rejects a book on the basis of its content in human experience, not because of its subtlety or its abstract esthetic values. In the last analysis, it is difficult to separate these things, since obviously form and content are part of the same whole. But it is interesting that when one asks even the most mature and perceptive of adolescents for the titles that have most significance in their reading, they choose books of extremely uneven literary merit. They place Exodus next to Crime and Punishment, or The Robe next to The Lord of the Flies. Furthermore, if one asks them why they chose particular books, the great majority of the replies deal with what the book was about. They were interested in the picture of a social problem represented; the book made them think of something they had not previously thought about; they were fascinated by the problems of human relations that the book presented. Only occasionally do they mention such things as the style of the language, the craftsmanship of the plotting, the aspects of characterization, the unity of all parts of the book toward a central theme.

5. So we come to the real crux of the matter. Young adults are reading adult literature, but not all adult literature. They are reading for content. What, then, are the areas of content for which they read? They idolize certain writers in each generation. What is the family relationship among these writers? In general their reading will fall into four large categories:

A. The Search. Young adults choose books in which individuals are looking for a direction for their lives. They are interested in characters caught in a value conflict, in a book in which value decisions are being formulated. Whether the book presents a resolution is not so important as the actual detailing of the search itself. Young adults of all generations and particularly of ours are desperately aware of the need to find significance in their own lives. Perhaps the decay of religious authority as a unifying force in our society and the ease with which the young person can find a job have accentuated the problem of coming to terms with oneself and one's life. "I have to find out who I am" is almost the slogan of the contemporary young adult. It is this theme, perhaps, more than any other that accounts for the fantastic popularity of Catcher in the Rye. Holden is on a pilgrimage to find himself: "Sex is one thing I don't understand. I swear to God I don't."

An old weak novel of Somerset Maugham's keeps turning up with great regularity among young adults' favorite books. It is The Razor's Edge, the story of a young man just out of the army who has a small legacy that means he doesn't have to work for the rest of his life. The book, then, becomes the search of the individual to decide what is worth doing with one's life when one has the freedom of decision that such a legacy makes possible. Of Human Bondage is one of the great and cherished reading experiences with this group. While it has several appealing themes, Philip's search for a value by which to lead his life is predominant. Graham Greene's A Burnt Out Case, with its picture of the individual who attempts to live "uninvolved" with anyone or anything, has the same quality of appeal. On a less mature level of writing, Howard Fast's April Morning and John Knowles' A Separate Peace are widely read for the pursuit of values involved in them.

B. Problems of the Social Order. Just as young people are involved with their own personal problems, they are also concerned with the problems of their society. Perhaps this is the crucial period in the individual's life in which he comes to terms with where he will stand in relation to his society. Thus, young people are interested in the book that deals with social injustices of prejudice, economic deprivation, or political tyranny. Books showing something of the problems of our political system or of the struggle of a people to find economic security and a place in the sun are almost inevitably favorites. Perhaps these books can be summed up by saying that almost any book showing deprived or persecuted people has appeal. As in all generations, imaginative literature seems to get closer to the heart than does the straight sociological treatment. Oscar Firkins once defined literature as "an idea with a glow." It is the internal glow that comes through to the reader so that the impersonal social situation becomes a personal problem involving each of us. In popular jargon, the reader can "connect." At the moment, books like <u>Advise and Consent</u>, <u>Black Like Me</u>, <u>Fail Safe</u>, <u>The Ugly American</u>, <u>1984</u> are prime favorites. Perhaps this theme, more than others in the book, accounts for the rather unexpected popularity of <u>To Kill a Mockingbird</u>.

C. The Bizarre, The Off Beat, The Unusual in Human Experience. Apparently, in looking for direction, the young adult is curious about the fringes of human life. Therefore, he seeks the book that details the strange and haunting human personality, the bizarre human experiences, the submerged recesses of human psychology and feeling. Often such books use strange and provocative symbols that are open to multiple interpretations, and therefore act as a sounding board against which the young reader can try out his own ideas and feelings. Perhaps no single book leaves a more lasting impression on the young adult than does Kafka's <u>Metamorphosis</u>, the utterly simple story of a man who finds himself changed into an enormous cockroach. They also enjoy Waugh's <u>The Loved One</u>, with its macabre satire of Hollywood burial customs. Conrad's <u>The Secret Sharer</u> is perhaps liked for these same reasons. <u>The Nun's Story</u> or <u>Crime and Punishment</u> intrigue the young person because they take him into unusual human activity. Each reader toys with the possibility of following where the heroes and heroines of these stories lead, even though briefly. I predict great readership for <u>Von Ryan's Express,</u> largely because the personality of Ryan is that of a man who acts in a pattern of behavior completely foreign to what most of us accept.

D. The Transition. Perhaps the single theme most sought by

the young adult is the book that details the movement of a character from adolescence into early adult life. One of my favorite devices has been a questionnaire in which I ask students to define the kind of book they would have an author write to order for them. A senior boy wrote that his would be "a book about a guy almost ready to leave home, but not quite. He doesn't know what he wants to do. His major interest is in his girl who lives in a city twenty-five miles away. His parents won't let him visit her except on the week ends. His other interest is in building hot rods." (It takes no great imagination to see that he is essentially describing the conditions and problems of his own life.) Then he concludes by saying that "I want the book written in such a way that he gets out of school, finds a job, gets married, and settles down."

Our culture has punctuation marks in an individual's life. Young adults are at perhaps the most salient one when they are deeply conscious of the fact that they must make the giant step from being a dependent member of society to being an independent one. So they choose books that at least suggest the ways that this master step is achieved. Sarah by Marguerite Bro and Maggi by Vivian Breck are eagerly read by the average junior or senior girl. Arrowsmith and Of Human Bondage, Great Expectations, The Way of All Flesh present similar themes for the more sophisticated. An exciting new book is Betty Smith's Joy in the Morning, showing with both realism and sentiment the problems of a young college couple in the first years of marriage.

Here then are the categories of literary experience in which most young adults select their reading, when it is available to them. Robert Whitman surveyed the National Achievement Award Winners in English for a three year period, 1960-1961-1962. These were young people in their senior year of high school and, for the most part, honors students and college-bound ones. They were asked to nominate a book, if there were such, that had greater significance for them than other books they had read. Almost a thousand students replied (37 per cent return) from all parts of the country. The list of the top forty books nominated substantiates the points that have been listed. The majority of the books were written during the twentieth century and most of the remaining ones during the latter half of the nineteenth century. The books can be neatly classified without exception under one of the four content areas. The Razor's Edge makes its appearance, as does Exodus. Also included are Thomas Wolfe, Ayn Rand, and, of course, Golding and Salinger.

These four themes—The Search, The Social Problem, The Unusual and The Transition—do not include the whole scope of literature by any means. In fact, the greatest themes of our most mature literature are not really included in them. Some of the themes that fall outside of young adult's reading but are nevertheless great themes of literature are:

A. The individual Caught In the Web of His Own Decisions. Perhaps real maturity is reached for the first time when one becomes deeply conscious that the decisions one makes set up turning points in one's life from which there is no retreat. The adolescent essentially lives in a world of "great possibilities" and he is always confident that alternatives will remain open to him. Otherwise, he wouldn't fight in a war or risk getting married or undertake the creation of a family or commit himself to a given major in college or accept a particular job offered him casually in a particular location. The awareness of the confines of life, by necessity, must come later to individuals. Out of it we realize the tragic nature of man. But this is not a theme for young people.

B. The Exploration of the Boundaries Within Which Life Can Be Lived. Built into the nature of man seems some intuitive sense that there is a proper sphere for man. If he tries to overstep the boundaries he is punished. The Greeks called it the operation of Nemesis. The exploration of these limits is one of the tremendous themes of great literature. Hawthorne used it endlessly, as did Melville and the Greek dramatists. The young adult has not lived through enough experiences to respond to it.

C. The Helplessness of Man against Cosmic Forces Indifferent to His Fate. The idea that life is perhaps an accidental kind of excrescence in the universal scheme of things haunts the mature mind. But how horrible if the young adult felt similarly! So he finds it hard to understand how Shakespeare could refer to men as flies that the gods kill for their sheer amusement. He has great difficulty in responding to a book like The Return of the Native. Even in a book like An American Tragedy he feels that Clyde Griffith made his own life and he refuses to feel sympathy for a person caught in the socio-economic determinism that Dreiser presents.

D. The Acceptance of Life's Limitations and Resignation to Them. A good deal of popular literature for the mature reader presents the quiet acceptance by the characters of what they are and the lives they are leading. The fires of rebellion have burned out and a simple dignity emerges for the person who has found what he is. Mary McCarthy's books are inclined toward this kind of picture of human beings. The golden dreams of youth have gone.

"For everything there is a season, and a time for everything under heaven."

When my daughter went to her first formal her favorite of favorite books was Gone with the Wind. The formals she now wears to college parties are quite sleek and different from the first pink nylon net one, and her reading tastes have moved considerably beyond Gone with the Wind. Someday she may need a gold lamé evening sheath and someday her reading interests will probably have matured beyond those of her present stage of growth. I do not think it was necessary to buy her a gold lamé sheath at fifteen so that she would know they exist. I do not think she needed to read King Lear or The Return of the Native at fifteen so that she would know they exist, when at thirty she might be ready to read them.

"For everything," surely, "there is a season, and a time for everything under heaven!"

"A Time and Season for the Better Reader" by Margaret Edwards. Top of the News, 21:229-235, April, 1965.

Shortly before the national election in November, a friend and I who were discussing the candidates for president agreed that one was obviously the more acceptable. In estimating the seemingly enormous following of the man we did not like, we wondered how there could be so many people in this nation who were not quite bright. Of course, the advocates of the other candidate were just as concerned for our sanity. But politics and jokes aside, it is a serious matter that so many people in this country are uninformed, uninspired, prejudiced, and thoughtless.

Right or wrong, we who live by the book believe that reading good books will inform, inspire, make for understanding, and stimulate thought. If this is true, we are not getting enough books in the hands of people at the age when they are most likely to form the habit of reading. I do not refer to books for school work. There, the record is better. Hordes of students are wearing out encyclopedias and bound magazines by constant use. We are ordering more and more books for them showing the structure of everything from the frog to the U.N. as well as supplying thousands of other books that supplement the course of study. With the resources available, most school and public librarians are doing a good job of enriching the curriculum. We are not doing so well in developing self-propelled readers.

In a community I once knew, where the cultural level was low, the young people, at the end of each school year, came to leave their cards on the librarian's desk saying, "School's out, Miss. I'm quitting." Without handing over the card or making the little speech, this is exactly the attitude of the majority of our teenagers. They have read books during their high school years in order to get good marks, to get into college, and to impress their teachers. At the end of high school, they "quit" because they see no reason for reading on their own. Why?

I believe there are two reasons:

(1) Administrators of both the public library and the public high schools are so overwhelmed by numbers and so pressed to provide essential materials for study that the matter of inculcating pleasure in reading, of getting people to read because they wish to read, seems unimportant in comparison with the ever-increasing demands of serious students. With hundreds of young people calling for reference materials and books to supplement the course of study, most administrators think they cannot afford the "luxury" of assigning a staff member to promote reading for pleasure—to discuss The Catcher in the Rye with a boy who wants to talk about it, or to laugh with him over The Education of Hyman Kaplan.

(2) Too many librarians who work with teenagers in school or public libraries have failed to make of themselves the readers they want teenagers to become. Readers are seldom created just by being in proximity to books. Nor are they created by pleasant librarians who offer assistance when asked for it. They are created and developed by contact with a person who makes the pursuit of reading seem stimulating and rewarding—who can discuss books and suggest reading the young person does not know exists or might not, on his own, have thought of reading. It is not a matter of waiting on the customer so much as stimulating him to read up to his potential and always with enjoyment.

To perform this service for the more mature, accelerated young adults who are likely to be the leaders and thinkers of the space age is as difficult as it is important, for the librarian must read faster, in greater depth, and on a wider variety of subjects than intelligent teenagers who themselves often read better than average adults. To illustrate this point, let us consider the four categories Dr. Carlsen[1] designated as being of most interest to better teenage readers.

1. "The Search"—Books that discuss the search for values central to the personality still trying to define itself—Who am I? What is it all about? What about the young adult who has already read The Catcher in the Rye, A Burnt-out Case, A Separate Peace, and April Morning? It is difficult to find many books that fit this category and,

at the same time, appeal to the young reader. One of the best is Baldwin's Go Tell It on the Mountain, in which a Negro boy looks back on the poverty, rejection, lovelessness of his life, reexamining the forces that shaped him and led him to throw himself before the altar in a mystic seizure. (Because teenagers are so interested in Baldwin and because he writes with a red hot pen, it is important for the librarian to read all his works and the reviews of them by reliable critics in order to discuss them intelligently with young readers. For example, Another Country should be understood by the teenager who has chosen to read it as a study of love in its various manifestations, especially the precarious love between the races. Otherwise the adolescent may see the book only as a sexy novel and wonder why Baldwin wrote it.)

All of us like Of Human Bondage, but few teenagers understand it. They think Philip a nut and do not realize that fate, in the end, put two keys to self-realization and happiness in his hand.

Salinger's Franny and Zooey belongs here. It is one of the best books I know for introducing the reader to literary criticism. A running gun battle on the Glass family using as ammunition the various contradictory estimates of the grown-up Quiz Kids and their emotional ordeal might start readers looking up reviews of other books they "discover."

I am not sure Miller's Death of a Salesman fits here, but if there is one philosophy the teenager has seen in operation, it is that of "being well liked," and this is an impressive study in trading integrity for popularity.

St. Exupery's Wind, Sand and Stars, with its musings on the meaning of life, has appeal for the very best readers. The chapter on Guillomet is full of the meaning, and the definition of man at the end of this chapter should be read by anyone shaping a philosophy. One of the things a young person has to learn is that one has to form his own individual philosophy, that he cannot take any man's philosophy in toto and, by it, find his way. He might understand how a personal philosophy is formed if he reads the page in John Canady's Mainstreams of Modern Art, where, in discussing the influences that played on Modigliani, he says, "But the most important factor in the compound of Modigliani's art is not Botticelli or African sculpture. Nor is it Ingres or the expressionists of the Sienese or Cezanne or Toulouse-Lautrec. It is Modigliani, an artist of creative talent, sensitive intelligence, and aesthetic discretion, who imitates none of these men or schools but fuses whatever he takes from them with his own perception of the world into an expressive art of great individuality."

2. "Problems of the Social Order"—Books on social values, on deprived and persecuted groups (Black Like Me, Fail Safe, The Ugly American, To Kill a Mockingbird).

The Hour is Late

How reassuring it is in these times, when juvenile delinquency is headlined and many despair of youth, to realize that it is the young people in this country who are combatting prejudice and injustice, even with their lives. The hour is late and our own cruelty may destroy us before the bomb falls. The matter is urgent enough that we must watch for effective magazine articles and call them, as well as books, to the attention of our readers. John Hersey's terrible article on trouble in Mississippi which appeared in the Saturday Evening Post, September 26, 1964, is important reading. Of course, there are many excellent books in this field. In Baldwin's The Fire Next Time, he pleads for understanding before the debacle. The last chapters of Steinbeck's Travels with Charley are so unbelievable, his publishers expected a suit. Anything Martin Luther King writes is important. Unfortunately, he does not have as much appeal for teenagers as Baldwin and more explosive writers. When I read Stride toward Freedom, I made plans to put it in the hands of my good readers and suggest that they follow it with a biography of Ghandi for an understanding of passive resistance and the sit-in. The idea did not work too well, possibly because the adolescent would rather identify with a suffering person than approach the problem philosophically.

The young adult who reads of unmerited suffering often asks for a reason. Ralph McGill, Daniels, and others have attempted to explain the trouble in the South but one of the most readable accounts is W. J. Cash's The Mind of the South. He attempts to show

how the rough frontiersman became the Southern aristocrat, developing hedonism and in the process a capacity for unreality, a love of rhetoric and fine speeches, a tendency to violence, and resentment of criticism. Baldwin, Langston Hughes, and others have shown us the cruelties of the North. This sadism practiced over the country is not peculiar to America, but is a symptom of the Nazi disease as the teenager can see when he reads Shirer's Rise and Fall of the Third Reich.

Nor is the active cruelty of the people in Europe and America the whole story. There is a passive cruelty which most of us practice, as Hochhuth has pointed out in The Deputy. Those very superior readers who would like to study modern man's inner mechanism might be able to read Erich Fromm's Escape from Freedom, in which an eminent psychoanalyst studies man, not a man, on his couch. In his discussion of the emotional development of modern man, he includes an analysis of Hitler and how he came to be.

Studies of values outside the field of race relations are of interest to better readers. Robert Jungk's Brighter Than a Thousand Suns explores the question on which Roshwald based Level 7. Jungk tells in readable style of the men who created the bomb and raises the problem of moral responsibility. We have long made use of Koestler's Darkness at Noon, the moving story of one Communist caught in the web of his devotion to the party and his pitiful efforts to justify himself the betrayals he had made for what had to be right. Pillai's Chemmeen is a haunting love story based on religious prejudice in India, and Markandaya's lovely Nectar in a Sieve shows how that nation's poverty allows only the most valiant and loving to survive in spirit.

Society's responsibility for the individual has been interpreted differently by many authors, and this is a question of concern to this generation. In Escape from Freedom, the author says that man's inclinations are not part of a fixed and biologically given human nature but result from the social process which creates man. Is this so, or is Mr. Golding right in saying man is inherently evil? Was society to blame, as Dreiser said it was in The American Tragedy and as Miller stated in The Cool World?

3. "The Bizarre, the Off-Beat, the Unusual in Human Experience"—(Kafka's Metamorphosis, Waugh's The Loved One, Rand's The Fountainhead).

In the annotation for Aristotle's Poetics in the Nioga Library System's fine College Preparatory Reading List, I found this: "Our Theatre of the Absurd, the building designs of Wright, Picasso's paintings, Britten's and Shostakovich's music, Camus' novels and plays and the plays of Albee and Beckett are not isolated works, but all are part of the indivisible artistic expression of our time." One of our most difficult tasks is to keep an open mind to the new and creative, and, at the same time, to remain honest enough not to pretend to like a book or a painting or a piece of music we really do not like after making a sincere effort to understand. The reader's advisor to the young adult should read widely in the field of the bizarre, the symbolic, the off-beat, and should encourage the young reader to do the same but should get over to him the idea that honest bewilderment is better than pretended enjoyment—that neither complete acceptance of everything nor wholesale condemnation is intelligent.

Understanding the "Despairing Men"

Martin Esslin's The Theatre of the Absurd explains the philosophy of the dramatists who believe man is lost (O Lost! Lost!), comparing them with the existentialists and discussing the personalities and the works of the major representatives of this school of thought. I could not discipline myself to complete the book, but I have a nodding acquaintance with these despairing men. I know what the word "absurd" means in this connotation, and I stand in amazement at Beckett, who "retained a terrible memory of life in his mother's womb" and wrote Waiting for Godot. Mr. Esslin explained Waiting for Godot so that I think I understand it. I wish I liked it. Esslin also discusses the relation of Camus to this group, but the best brief basis for a discussion for his The Stranger and The Plague can be found in the annotation for The Fall in the N.C.T.E. Committee's The College and Adult Reading List.

Bertolt Brecht, as that same list suggests, was "a flexible

and original artist (who) sought new form in an effort to realize a new concept of theater." His Mother Courage, with its cynical depiction of war, centers, as the introduction to a collection says, ". . . around a negative, passive, cowardly woman content to flow with the tide though it leads to death." "The Song of the Wise and Good" is so delightfully wicked, it is my favorite of all the original and clever songs in the play. While the play shows Brecht for the innovator he was, another dramatist made a good try at a cynical depiction of war, with women at the center. He too had good songs along with humor and a good deal of sex. Aristophanes called his play Lysistrata.

Among the many charming, original works in this field, we think of The Glass Menagerie, The Grass Harp, The Green Pastures, Japanese Haichu and such collections of Chinese verse as Waley has edited.

Knowing the appeal of Ayn Rand for young adults, I recently read her Anthem, which the blurb says "presents a key to the world's moral crisis." The key, as I interpret it, turns out to be the philosophy that man's greatest moral duty is the pursuit of his own happiness. It seems to me quite important that the librarian for young adults read popular authors with "keys" and "messages"—not to attempt to convert the reader to one's own point of view, but to be sure the young person understands what the author is saying.

For those confused and bewildered by some of the unhappy, mixed-up authors, there is some balm of Gilead in Joseph Wood Krutch's article which many of us read in the May 9, 1964, issue of the Saturday Review of Literature, "Confessions of a Square."

4. "Transition"—(The character moves from adolescence into early adult life).

Joyce's Portrait of the Artist as a Young Man is not easy reading. There is sex but no love and the appeal is more intellectual than passionate, as we follow an Irish youth (obviously Joyce) as he outgrows his family, his school, his church, and even Irish politics to set out for the continent, where he will think his own thoughts. Malamud's The Natural depicts a youth moving into adult life who makes the wrong turn in the road because his sense of values is false. Willa Cather's <u>My Antonia</u> and <u>Lucy Gayheart</u> belong here, but while Cather writes simply, what she has to say often escapes young readers. Thomas Wolfe seems never to have completed his transition from adolescence to maturity, but he wrote eloquently of his long journey.

Though Dr. Carlsen mentioned only fiction in setting up this category, the transition to maturity has been remembered and written about appealingly by Moss Hart, Margaret Bourke-White, Ernest Gann, Agnes De Mille, and Jesse Stuart. None of them writes a more moving autobiography than the ugly, unloved, lonely Eleanor Roosevelt who grew into the most loved and beautiful woman in the world.

The advanced, accelerated reader will read almost anything the librarian reads if the librarian has gained the young person's confidence and has earned his respect by the variety and quality of his own reading. The specific titles mentioned in this article certainly will not appeal to every good reader. In fact, given to the wrong reader at the wrong time, they may kill him off. The books have been mentioned in an attempt to give a few "for instances" in thinking how we might deal with those older, better readers who have already read the obvious titles. Each of us has his own special problems, his own arsenal of useful tools, and his own best judgment of "seasons" in reading.

Conclusion

In our zeal to inspire and enrich our more intelligent, more mature readers, we may be carried away. Let us remember that these readers are rare, that they are more likely to go to college and learn to run on their own steam than our other readers. I do not mean to discount the importance of whetting the appetite of these accelerated young people for the best reading, but the American public is still the bailiwick of the public school and the public library and this public is made up largely of unread, unawakened, uninspired young people who are innocent of books and reading. There is no greater service we can perform than to inculcate in the masses of teenagers a love of reading, and this is often done with a teenage romance, a simple, warm, love story or historical novel, or books about space, sports, cars.

If we can teach the unawakened that reading is a delight and the library is a fine place to go, we may eventually turn out a respectable number of readers in this country and help leaven the lump of apathy and provincialism here. The young adult librarian's job consists of reading for all levels, from the most deprived and reluctant to the accelerated; in knowing when it is time for Now That I'm Sixteen and when for Mother Courage; in working to bring each reader, on his own, to read up to his potential. This theme— "For everything there is a season, and a time for everything under heaven."—ran through Dr. Carlsen's wonderful talk.

Notes

1. Carlsen, G. Robert. "For Everything There Is a Season," Top of the News, January, 1965.

"Promoting Adolescent Growth Through Reading" by
Geneva R. Hanna. Education, 84:472-475, April, 1964.
Reprinted with the permission of The Bobbs-Merrill
Company, Inc.

Book bannings and burnings attest to the fact that we of the Western world have great faith in the power of the printed word. Research evidence in this area as yet is inconclusive, but there are enough findings supporting the belief to indicate that there is some truth in it.

If books can have negative effects upon the minds of men, then surely they can have positive effects. A sense of identification with a successful man or woman, a feeling of sympathy and even compassion for one who is suffering, a reaction of honest indignation at an injustice done to another—these are all common responses individuals experience while reading. These reactions will have some kind of impact upon the individual.

Self-understanding and self-acceptance are essential ingredients for the child or young person growing toward maturity. Both are difficult to acquire. For many children reading may be one of the chief sources for experimenting with life or for discovering that other people have similar problems that may be met and solved.

Children need to learn while still quite young that all families have problems to solve, that each member has something to contribute, and that they are happiest when they are being themselves and accepting themselves as responsible members of a family group. Estes helps children identify with this kind of family situation in The Moffats, as does Stolz for adolescent girls in Pray Love, Remember or Moody in Little Britches for older adolescents.

Other needs such as the person feeling that he is like everyone else and that he is accepted by his peer group are also important if children and young people are to develop into mature, stable, thinking adults. These are problems which children are frequently loath to discuss with adults because most adults have long forgotten how very important these "trivial" matters are to the growing, developing young person.

Frequently young people gain much consolation and real understanding through seeing similar problems disturbing the hero or heroine in a story and in living vicariously with him as he seeks to solve them with greater or lesser success. Boys will identify with Rickey in Felsen's Street Rod as he seeks to provide himself with the crowd's status symbol—a car—and as he strives in many misguided ways to be first, always, to be "the" leader.

The older boy will see himself in several aspects of the confused striving of Holden Caulfield, the principal character of Salinger's much discussed and controversial Catcher in the Rye. Simply being able to say, "That is just the way I felt at such and such a time," or "I thought I was the only one who ever reacted like that," gives any person the momentary feeling of belonging to the human race, a warm feeling of assurance that one is not a strange, foreign being, but much like others. This sense of belonging, of feeling secure because others have also suffered or had doubts or been rejected helps build a sense of personal worth and can lead on into more sympathetic understanding and acceptance of others, given proper encouragement and help.

For most people the act of reading almost any type of human experience is a kind of role playing. They identify with certain characters, empathize with them, live their lives, react with them, and for a little while become those persons. If the reading material is at the proper level of difficulty so that it is both challenging and understandable, if it captures their attention and then piques their curiosity, it is bound to have some impact on them.

Readiness Important

No one can predict with accuracy which experiences will affect the individual most. We know that readiness is important. All readers at times in their reading discover materials—stories, essays, poems—which suddenly seem to give perspective and insight, to integrate life's experiences as nothing else has. Ideas, cause and effect relationships, understandings which previously have escaped one, suddenly become clear and obvious. When this happens the reader feels he has discovered a great book, a magnificent poem, a brilliant essay.

However, read at an earlier or later time in his life, this same book might not have impressed him so dramatically. The time was right, the reading experience furnished what he was seeking, and he suddenly became a more mature, insightful human being because he read a certain story.

Awareness of Social Problems

Reading can help children and young people become more aware of the social problems of the world in which they live. At first the naive reader may be more attracted by the differences, the oddities in the world across the tracks or in another country, than he is in finding out why things are different. Gradually, as he becomes more accustomed to different ways of behaving, he often begins to realize that it is mainly the outward manifestation of behavior which is different and that basically we are much more alike than we are different. Questions eventually arise from the reading as to why persons behave differently and these questions can often lead to deeper searching and more satisfying answers as the individual matures.

The young reader who has read avidly the Lois Lenski books or those by such authors as Phyllis Whitney or Florence Means is bound to have developed at least some empathy for children of minority cultural groups or those whose families earn their livings in less familiar ways, such as the migratory workers.

Biographies Open New Worlds

Biographies of famous people often open up new worlds to their readers. It would be difficult to read the life of Albert Schweitzer of Tom Dooley without gaining a new admiration for men who have the compassion and devotion to humanity to give up successful material careers in order to minister to the physical and spiritual needs of the ignorant and destitute. The life of Ghandhi has the power to make those who read about him a little more humble and dedicated to the cause of mankind. The lives of men like Lincoln and Kennedy make one realize how difficult it is to know what is "right," yet how important it is to do "as God gives us to see the right."

Frequently children and young people have no concept of the problems and hardships persons whom they admire have faced and somehow overcome or learned to live with. Even the lives of persons of lesser stature can often help build understandings—people like Babe Ruth, Jackie Robinson, Jesse Stuart, or Billie Burke, who have overcome economic or racial problems in their climb to success.

Reading Fills the Gaps

Knowledge about the way people live and their problems and difficulties is important. Without information, no understanding can be built, and without understanding there can be no interpretation and no action. Reading about prejudice and discrimination against minority groups, or the problems of labor and management, or the needs of migratory workers may furnish valuable background about the needs of society.

In the present era of rapid transportation and instantaneous communication it is possible to rub elbows with many more people and to know firsthand how other people live and how they feel about what happens to them. There is less excuse for provincialism than there was before World War II. However, much that is seen and heard is viewed or heard hastily and superficially without sufficient background to produce understanding or considered judgment. Reading materials are still important to help fill in the gaps of information, to furnish detail and further evidence, to help interpret what is seen first hand.

Guidance Important

This information may open new areas of interest and concern for the young reader, but this is not sufficient. Books of and by themselves can only serve as informers and stimulators. It is the reader who must interpret the experience and make it meaningful. Only the reader can build his own socially sensitive attitudes and grow into a mature adult.

The act of integration of information into socially sensitive attitudes is seldom accomplished without much guidance from intelligently aware adults. This guidance is of tremendous importance, but

The Adolescent and His Reading

it is also the most difficult to administer with sufficient wisdom to help the young reader. Telling the young person what to think concerning what he reads or observes is no help. It only makes him dependent upon adult judgment or rebellious of it.

Children and adolescents must learn to think for themselves. But with no guidance they often come to unsound conclusions or make rash or even dangerous decisions. Young people have been known to start revolutions because of some real or imagined injustice they have experienced or read about. Tom Paine has been given much credit for stirring up feeling among the young colonists by his tract <u>Common Sense.</u> We want men who can be aroused to action, but we also want men who temper right with justice and who seek to solve problems not rashly or dangerously but with wisdom and compassion.

Guidance which promotes personal and social growth as a result of reading must be done subtly and with a light touch. The objective is to help young people learn how to solve their own problems and the problems of society with intelligence and wisdom.

The adult thus engaged must forego the desire to tell them what to think and when and how to act. This is not a simple process. As a prerequisite, the adult engaged in such guidance must first of all know much about the children and young people with whom he is working as well as the society and the world in which they live. Besides this, he must know firsthand the materials the young people are reading in order to know what the author has really said, what the implied problems are, and what the possible interpretations might be. He must allow the young person complete freedom of honest reaction.

Probably the most effective technique in reading guidance is that of raising questions in order to push understandings to greater depths and interpretations to more significant levels. These understandings and interpretations may seem somewhat superficial to the adult, but their importance must be measured in terms of the growth level of the individual, not in terms of customary arbitrary adult standards.

Growth Toward Maturity

Growth toward maturity is the ultimate aim of reading, especially growth in the ability to understand and accept oneself and others and to face and solve social problems with some effectiveness. As long as growth is evident, as long as insights of greater significance are developing, as long as the reading undertaken is aiding in the individual's ability to think things through rationally, progress is being made. Then it really matters little whether the growth has occurred as a result of reading Alice in Wonderland or The Red Badge of Courage; what really matters is that personal and social growth can and has taken place through reading.

If this happens often enough to the young person as a result of his reading, he will become a reader, and what is even more important, he will become a mature, adequately adjusted, and socially responsible adult.

"Needed: More Literature Reading" by Hazel C. Hart. Education, 84:339-341, February, 1964. Reprinted with the permission of The Bobbs-Merrill Company, Inc.

A well-organized curriculum provides many opportunities for children to read and to enjoy quality literature, just as it provides for instruction in the various content areas.

All types of reading—developmental, informational, and literary reading—are recognized as essential. Each serves specific functions. Literary reading has many values, one of which is to help the children come to appreciate the choicest materials available for them to read.

Reading Environment Essential

It is recognized today, as never before, that home, school, and library should assume greater responsibilities in fostering and nurturing the love of reading. Much can be accomplished by giving children early exposure to literature—by helping them to sense and to experience the actual enjoyment that may come from books.

A number of research studies have shown that enthusiasm for literature on the part of a parent or teacher is contagious. One recent researcher found a direct connection between a teacher's reading books aloud to children and their growing interest in books. In many instances children sought to obtain and to examine the same books and to have the books read over and over again. Also, some of the children used similar art media in depicting incidents from the stories in the books.

Effects of Deprivation

Other research studies show that children from depressed, meager homes often are linguistically backward. This is especially true in homes where no oral reading is provided and few if any books are found. It must be noted, however, that linguistic retardation does not necessarily indicate mental backwardness.

The deprivation of reading and books is not altogether confined to homes in the lower socio-economic bracket. Surveys of homes in higher socio-economic brackets reveal that relatively little time is devoted to family reading, which once was the bread and butter of family living.

What happens to children who have little or no opportunity to experience the effects of fine literature? The answer is obvious—by and large these are the children who lack appreciation of the accuracy and beauty of language. It is a sad commentary when children are given no opportunity to develop an understanding or appreciation of the English language which they speak.

Reading and Other Media

Today reading has to compete with other popular communication media, as television, radio, and movies. These media appeal to persons of all ages and in many respects serve the same purposes as reading. They make heavy inroads into the time that might be devoted to reading, doubtless far out of proportion to the values derived.

Reading has many important advantages over these other communication media. First, it provides a greater variety of content, permitting a person to reach out and obtain materials that he wants or needs. Secondly, reading is adjustable. The reader can set the pace at which he reads. He can accelerate his reading when he comes to materials that are familiar or easily understood, and he can slow down when he comes to materials that are new or difficult.

Contributions of Literature

Literature affords children contact with an opportunity to extend their vocabularies. Many words, although new at first, are taken over and used until they become old friends. Attuning the ear to the preciseness and beauty of an author's words develops sensitivity in the selection and use of words. This sensitivity grows as the child grows older.

Literature helps children to enrich content fields, whetting their appetites for more specific information. It helps them to develop new interests in science, in social studies, and other areas of the curriculum. Pushing out boundaries by exploring new interests, reading diversified materials, increasing acquaintance with source books are thrilling experiences for the child. The outcomes are certain to bring about greater power in reading with corresponding development of such attendant skills as critical, analytical, and creative reading.

Literature contributes greatly to personality development. Children develop personality when they have something to say and can say it competently and confidently. Contributing experiences include the discussion of stories, retelling of stories, dramatization, puppetry, and all the other language arts activities associated with the reading of stories and poems.

Literature strengthens children's abilities to mingle with other persons. The communication of ideas in a social setting involves varied purposes for communicating, varied types of communication, careful selection of words, phrases, and sentences. Children gradually develop social skills when they begin to realize that the best way to solve social and economic problems is to analyze situations carefully before reaching decisions. They can analyze situations more readily if they possess the necessary language skills to communicate effectively.

Literature gives children an insight into human nature. It affords them an opportunity to meet vicariously many book characters like themselves, and others vastly different from themselves. They come to see how book characters live, work, and play, solve problems, have fun, and suffer frustrations. In many instances they come to look upon these characters as real flesh-and-blood people. Thus reading contributes a measure of comfort to readers and helps them to feel that their own problems or concerns are less staggering than they might otherwise be.

Literature provides a means of escape from the world of reality. Everyone, whether old or young, feels the need at times to free himself from the shackles of commonplace affairs and to extend his wings and soar far, far away. Thus literature helps to relieve tensions and emotions and serves as a stabilizing force.

Summary

Today as never before emphasis should be placed on the great contribution that literature makes in helping children to grow intellectually, socially, and emotionally. Never in the history of the world has there been greater need for increased ability to communicate effectively and efficiently with other people in order to reap the benefits of appreciation and sympathetic understanding.

Sensitively written literature is needed by children much as they need food for daily living. Home, school, and library must combine to instill in children a love of books, a respect for their mother-tongue, and a desire to learn to speak and to write well.

We applaud all those who through conscientious efforts have achieved, in some measure at least, the ultimate goal of stimulating boys and girls to become book-loving children.

Heads up! Forward march! On the double! Parents, educators, and librarians—literature must be given its rightful place!

Part Two. Fiction for the Adolescent

"The Novel in the High School Library" by Lois Blau, Wisconsin Library Journal, 60:178-181, May, 1964. Reprinted with the permission of the publisher.

A school library has only one reason for existing—to assist in the education of our young people. The school library must enrich the curriculum with supplementary books in all subject fields, thus enabling the teacher and the students to survey all facets of a given problem, and to arrive at a more critical appraisal of that problem. Books, magazines, newspapers, pamphlets, visual aids— all are grist to that mill, and all have a place and a part in the school library's partnership with the school.

A library must also offer those books which enrich the life of the student, and which help him to become a well-rounded, imaginative, creative adult. The education of the whole child is our goal. We must help him to develop intellectually as he grows—to enlarge his horizons with the magic, the fun, the wisdom presented by the great minds of the past and the present. Fairy tales, legends, myths, sagas, epics, novels—all of these are stepping stones to understanding the human comedy.

Of all the forms of literature, perhaps the novel is the most significant in the cultural education of the young adults. Certainly it is the most controversial, and the area in which we feel the most pressure to select, or censor, or whatever term you choose to use. A statement in the book Reading Ladders for Human Relations, by Heaton and Lewis, clearly articulates the reason. "The novel offers readers an opportunity to identify emotionally with human beings who are in interaction with their fellows. It provides access to the feelings of other people in a way otherwise offered only by face-to-face contacts. . . it also offers readers concrete, living examples of human behavior and relationships. (The novel) provides occasion for mulling over, interpreting, comparing, and contrasting responses. By this analysis the reader gains insight and understanding of principles that apply to his own experience."

Most of us realize that in this modern day we cannot keep all lurid, sensational influences out of the reach of our young people. We cannot remove mention of sex, when paperback books offer (among the wonderful choices) other selections which contain more graphic passages than any novel we might have on our shelves. The questions we ask ourselves in the matter of selection or censorship might be as follows: How many adult novels are suitable to be placed upon the shelves of a high school library? How much criticism can we expect, and stand up to, when we put a controversial novel into the hands of our high school students? What do we owe our young people in mature judgments on our part, concerning the sort of literature which we think will last, and not be of transient value, which will stir the imagination, being full of truth and not false values?

I believe that high school librarians must take the responsibility for having the best literature on the shelves, both classic and modern. I think we must have novels in the tradition of Butler's Way of All Flesh, Maugham's Of Human Bondage, Joyce's Portrait of the Artist as a Young Man, and Salinger's Catcher in the Rye. Ernest Pontifex, Philip Carey, Joyce, and Holden Caulfield are all young men with problems of family conflict (sic), misunderstandings, and gropings after truth. Such characters in such situations have a poignant meaning for most adolescents, who can see in the lives of these young men their own insecurities mirrored. One of our high school students wrote, on The Catcher in the Rye: "If I were a writer, I would like very much to have the qualities of Mr. J. D. Salinger. . . I cannot remember reading a story of any type which brought out thoughts so perfectly as this book. They were common thoughts and ideas expressed so as to give you a feeling of security. They were so much like your very own, which you were afraid to admit, for fear they were different. . ."

Adolescents enjoy also the verbosity of Thomas Wolfe, filled with poetry and imagery as it is. . .a revelation to the intelligent boy or girl who reads of the commonplace Gant family with the more wonder since it has produced not only frantic, foolish, exciting

Fiction for the Adolescent   47

Eugene, but also gentle Ben. And what of <u>All Quiet on the Western Front</u>, <u>A Farewell to Arms</u>, and <u>A Walk in the Sun</u> which bring the grief of war home to our young people through the calm acceptance of its horrors. What of Faulkner's <u>Miss Emily</u>, <u>The Bear</u>, and <u>The Spotted Horses</u>; in drama, why not <u>The Dark at the Top of the Stairs</u>, or <u>A Raisin in the Sun</u>, for succinct sermons against prejudice and racial hatreds? These books are filled with life and immediacy, and so appeal to the teen-ager of today, conditioned as he is to the action and quick denouncement of the movie and television dramas.

From Shakespeare to Salinger, from Horace to Hemingway—we must have them all on our shelves if we are to call ourselves librarians, and call our place of business a library. This is no time to fail our students because of fear of bigotry, of ignorance, of political demagogery. Unless we can place our profession in the front of this battle against censorship, we will fail in our aim—that of giving to the young people the best literature in the world. . . books considered as a whole, not picked apart by those who say that isolated passages will corrupt the young. Another of our students wrote a poem which to my mind illustrates this point beautifully.

> "One twisted, bare tree limb
> Is nothing by itself.
> But as part of a tree
> It is beautiful. . ."

We have a job to do, and the tools to do it. We do not stand alone in this matter of censorship and its effects. Our professional organizations have laid it on the line for all the world to see. The National Council of Teachers of English has given us the statement "The Students' Right to Read." The American Library Association's "Library Bill of Rights," "The School Library Bill of Rights," "The Freedom to Read Statement" all are at our side.

I believe that each of us must face up to this question of selection and censorship in our own particular library. I think we must have the courage of our convictions, and that we must acquire those convictions for which we will need that courage. I do not think that it will do for us to be timid, or fearful, or dependent upon others to make our decisions for us. This is a time when we must give our young people no less than the best, for they may have decisions to make which will require all the courage and fortitude and wisdom which we can offer them through the great minds of the past and the present.

Let us help them to build a better world by bringing up a generation which is not afraid of the truths of life; which can be strong, yet compassionate—ready for a world full of conflicts and hatreds which can only be resolved by the insight and the courage which comes from knowledge and understanding.

"To Sail Beyond the Sunset" by G. Robert Carlsen.
The English Journal, 42:297-302, 330. September, 1953.
Reprinted with the permission of the National Council
of Teachers of English.

> . . . for my purpose holds
> To sail beyond the sunset, and the baths
> Of all the western stars. . . .
> Tennyson

Like a golden thread, adventure runs through the history of literature, sometimes achieving the status of immortality and sometimes degenerating into a simple series of local and peculiar incidents. Adventure is chance, a remarkable occurence, a bold undertaking, a stirring action. Man's interest in such tales is not a casual and merely entertaining pastime. For all individuals need to test themselves to find the limits of their capacities. Adolescents, particularly, still climb on the undersides of bridges or drive a car as fast as they dare on a dangerous stretch of road or bum their way across the country and around the world mainly to find out the kind of stuff of which they are made. This kind of testing takes place within books as well, for we like to see, even though vicariously, of what our species is made.

When one first thinks of the adventure story written for the teen-age boy, one remembers the books of the early part of the twentieth century: Treasure Island, Prester John, Lance of Kanana, The Dark Frigate, Spice and the Devil's Cave, The Trumpeter of Krakow, and the like. These books seemed to us of an older generation the very essence of adventure, excitement, romance; in our memory, the more recent stories pale into insignificance.

Even though it is not completely right to lump such diverse titles together and to make generalizations, there is some strange similarity in quality about them. All of them have an aura of romance and mystery cast over them from a peculiar kind of style, a choice of words, or a magic sentence structure. The language suggests a withdrawal from the world of ordinary life into a world almost but not quite of imagination. Perhaps this can be seen at a glance from a few of the early lines in several of these books:

> I remember him as if it were yesterday, as he came plodding to the inn door, his sea-chest following behind him in a handbarrow; a tall, strong, heavy, nut-brown man; his tarry pigtail falling over the shoulders of his soiled blue coat; his hands ragged and scarred, with black broken nails, and the saber cut across one cheek, a dirty, livid white (Treasure Island).

> I mind as if it were yesterday my first sight of the man. Little I knew at the time how big the moment was with destiny, or how often that face seen in the fitful moonlight would haunt my sleep and disturb my waking hours (Prester John).

> The name of Kanana is still a magic battle cry among the sons of Ishmael and his lance is one of the most precious relics of Arabia (Lance of Kanana).

One is struck, too, with the dependence in these older books on the magic of place names. In Spice and the Devil's Cave, a finger is "traced along the bulge of Africa's West Coast." Arabia, India, the Marquesas Islands, New Guinea, and Timbuktu spelled the unusual, the unknown, and, consequently, the field for unusual actions.

Most of the older adventure stories revolve around struggles between two or more groups of men. In most cases, these are good men and bad men. The bad men have traveled to the far corners of the earth or have come from little-known parts of the world and, as a consequence, possess strange kinds of intuition and often occult magic. Notice it particularly in Treasure Island. The old seamen stalk into the Admiral Benbow Inn one after the other. They are mysterious figures with strange and mysterious knowledge collected from the distant parts of the world. They have physical defects: scars, blindness, a peg leg; almost instinctively we know they are up to no good; while the good, clean-living and stay-at-home English doctor and Jim Hawkins himself are obviously "right-minded." And, sure enough, that is the way they line themselves up in the story. Prester John is full of such classifications of characters. You shudder at the description of the Negro in the first chapter, and the natives later on in the story are obviously addicts to strange rites. They are a race of people with primitive and savage intuitive powers

Fiction for the Adolescent   51

not remembered by the civilized man from western Europe. Such power goes with villainy. The fight then is one between two opposing forces of men, and the issue is almost always painted as black and white. The reader is left in no doubt about which side is which, though in many cases the ethical problem aroused seems resolved in favor of those having the least legal right in the situation. While certainly this generalization is not true of all the adventure stories of the period, it is true enough to merit attention, particularly since it underlies the two most frequently read: <u>Treasure Island</u> and <u>Prester John</u>.

    A further rather general characteristic is the use of the past as a means of evoking wonder and awe. "I take up my pen in the year of grace, 17__," says Stevenson. <u>Lance of Kanana</u> happens, to all intents and purposes, before the dawn of history. The authors use dim and shadowy times, not to bring them keenly alive before the minds of readers, but as a kind of separation or a withdrawal into the realm of adventure.

    In these books the daily and routine concerns of man are omitted. There is an occasional mention made of sweeping a room or reading a book; but, basically, the characters live their lives in the white heat of adventure, untrammeled by the physical necessities of daily life. I find it extremely annoying in <u>Treasure Island</u> to have a group of mundane businessmen run up to London, buy a boat, outfit it, and hire a crew of sailors, without any explanation of how they managed to raise the money. But such are not concerns in these stories.

    In most of these books, setting and characterization are of little importance. In essence, the assumption seems to be that the names of distant places conjure up enough without any necessity of detailing the quality of the background. Basically, the characters are a pretty stickish sort of being, with labels put on them. Occasionally the outside of a person comes to life, but very seldom do we find out anything about personality beyond whether the individual is right-minded or power-mad. Even Long John Silver is a rather vague figure when you really come down to looking at what is in the book instead of letting the motion-picture image of him confuse the issue. Action, action, and more action is what constitutes these books, and our fondness for them lies in our liking for the rather artificial flow of language in which the action is recounted.

History has not dealt kindly with the materials of which these books were made. The dependence on the names of remote parts of the globe to conjure up romance and unusual happenings, to give the reader a mind-set, has all but vanished into thin air. An island off the coast of South America is "on the run" of sister who is an airline hostess. The Solomons, Guadalcanal, New Guinea, no longer seem remote. A group of teachers from the school hop a plane for Africa during the vacation. The world has grown infinitely smaller, and familiarity has bred contempt. It no longer is enough to sail to the South Pacific to expect adventure to happen. We know the South Pacific from the accurate pictures that we saw when we were studying the islands.

Similarly, the never-never land of history has blown away to a certain extent. The boy today is interested in history, but not as a cloudy mist to veil the reality of a situation. He wants his history to evoke for him a living age of real people and to show him relations with the present.

Perhaps the reader can still accept the classification of people into good and bad and the stereotyping of people by occupation, race, and religion; but it goes against the grain to encourage young people to read books with such misconceptions in them.

Writers today have had, as a consequence, to find adventure in different themes. One of the most interesting changes in the recent group of books has been the moving-away from themes dealing with a conflict between men to themes of the conflict between nature and man. Perhaps modern man, living each generation in a more civilized and controlled kind of environment, needs assurance that he could still adjust himself to rougher environments. There are several recurrent themes: mountain-climbing and skiing; life in the deep woods; the struggle against extreme heat or cold; the mystery of the sea; and the most interesting and exciting, the struggle against infinite space quite outside the known world. Literally, the books are sailing beyond the sunset.

Fiction for the Adolescent   53

Montgomery Atwater, an official in the Forest Service, has written frequently of the struggles of a young man serving in the control and conservation of our forests. The Hank Winton books, for example, detail the record of Hank in his entrance into two branches of the service. Here is adventure in which the major opponent is the treachery of nature through which the forests are dried mercilessly by the sun, so that the least touch of lightning may set off a conflagration. Young Hank deliberately sets out to fight such happenings, isolating himself on a mountain lookout in one of the books and, in another, becoming a smoke-jumper, willing to catapult himself into the midst of a burning area and pit his strength and intelligence against the whims of the flame and wind. Certainly such a theme is every bit as exciting as the struggle of Jim Hawkins against Long John and the convicts. In a way, nature here has many of the same traits of character as does Long John—in one mood, affable, smiling, thoroughly lovable; in the next completely treacherous. Lathrop's Northern Trail Adventure, while having a conflict between men within it, becomes of greatest significance in its detailing of the adjustment of men to the ruggedness of the North. The human villains pale to insignificance in comparison with the subtle treachery of the Yukon winter, where the characters face loneliness, storm, the threat of sudden thaws, and blinding blizzards in their effort to live.

Robert DuSoe's Three without Fear sets a similar stage, but at the opposite extemes of climatic conditions. Three teen-agers, two Mexicans and an American, are thrown together in the heat and desert of Lower California. The story concerns their nomadic wandering of the full length of the peninsula, until they finally find human beings who will care for them. They face the sea; they learn how to make nature feed them; they suffer thirst; they suffer illness and utter fatigue, as they move laboriously north up the great and gaunt stretch of land. Their opponent becomes a clear-cut character, almost a tangible thing. Armstrong Sperry deals with the struggle against nature also. Sometimes it is the sea, as in Hull Down for Action and in his finest book, Call It Courage; another time it is the ruggedness of the jungle, in The Rain Forest. In Hull Down for

Action, he pits four men on an open raft against the immensity of the Pacific, moving only by the mysterious currents of the sea.

The interest in the mountains is relatively new in adventure stories. Stephen Meader, in Behind the Ranges, details the excitement and charm of the mountains but does little with them in the action of his story. Arthur Stapp accomplishes more in this area, particularly in Mountain Tamer, where the fear of mountains is a major theme in the story of a boy who sets out deliberately to conquer himself. Stapp, again, does not quite make of the mountains the exciting opponent they might be. Probably most successful, though not writing for boys, is Vivian Breck, who, in High Trail, pits the ruggedness of the mountains squarely against her heroine. There is the beauty and solemnity of the mountains and all their treachery. Very recently, the French writer Frison-Roche (First on a Rope) dealt with the same kind of theme of men and mountains. His writing about mountains and their moods and grandeur, however, far outdistances his writing about human beings, and consequently the books do not become exciting adventures. One rather wonders why man wins in the end.

Probably the finest of the treatments of nature-and-man adventures for the teen-age boy is Paul Annixter's Swiftwater. Here is a boy thrown into his father's job as a trapper in the dead of winter because his father has fallen and broken his leg. Starting out alone he spends nights in the woods; he is attacked by a cougar; he knows intense cold and the loneliness of the deep forest, but also he knows the satisfaction of proving that he can do it. From his struggle with nature, his love of nature deepens as his personality matures.

The new element of nature in the adventure books is outer space. From the many rather cheap accounts written on demand from the publishers, one writer has emerged who treats his theme seriously. Though the Heinlein books are uneven in level, they are uniformly satisfying in the treatment of the relation between man and space. Heinlein never lets his reader forget the puniness of man, and he has great sensitivity to the size and magnitude of nature, this time on a universal scale. The treachery of space is met time after time with the fortitude and courage of the human speck, until the

Fiction for the Adolescent   55

marks of man are all over the galaxy. Here is a master-theme, handled with nice sensitivity to the philosophical aspects of the situation as well as to the adventure.

When the adventure story focuses on the relation of man to nature, setting immediately becomes of immense importance. One of the heartening things about the kind of stories that have been mentioned is the depth of the writers' appreciations, their subtle understanding of colors, sounds, nuances, and moods in nature. And yet, by the fact that the theme of the story makes of nature a character, there is always an integration of action and background, so that passages do not intrude as purple splotches impeding the stories. Here is one dimension found in the present adventure story that was almost totally lacking from those of the past. If we have sacrificed the appealing rhythms and magical spell of the style of Prester John, we have gained a depth of beauty in the delineation of the natural habitat of man.

But we have gained far more; for in the present books the interest has shifted from a sheer sequence of action to the effect of the action on the lives of the people involved. Jim Hawkins seems to have skimmed through his pursuit of buried treasure without growing or changing in any way whatsoever, and David Crawford in Prester John does not react to his experiences of quelling a rebellion of natives. Perhaps the difference is best seen in Armstrong Sperry's Call It Courage. Here a boy, born on a South Pacific island, has, through near drowning, become afraid of the water. Because of his fears he becomes an outcast and a coward. The adventure begins when he finally takes himself in hand and, alone in an outrigger, sets sail for the island inhabited by the enemies of his people. Through deliberately facing danger and through his fight with a shark, he not only wins prestige but also overcomes his fear. There are adventure and excitement of the highest kind in the book, but they are tied together by the personality of the character and become a rich and satisfying literary experience.

This kind of theme runs through book after book. Stapp, in Mountain Tamer, uses much the same theme, perhaps not quite so subtly. Shannon Garst, in Cowboy Boots, treats the West in a similar vein. Here is the thrill of ranch life in the modern West; but it is held together by the attempts of a rather irresponsible boy to meet the demanding requirements of his uncle. Annixter's Swiftwater treats magnificently the theme of maturation through a boy's assumption of the responsibilities of running his father's trap lines. The adventure is the experience that subtly matures the hero. Louise Rich's Start of the Trail deals with a similar experience in the life of a young Maine guide. His love of the woods is pitted against his disrespect for and his hatred of school. He holds himself slightly superior to the "dudes" whom he guides, because of their abysmal ignorance of the simple facts of life in the open. Through the adventures that are his that summer, he comes to see both people and school in a different perspective.

Howard Pease has done this kind of thing in many books. In Heart of Danger, he tells an espionage story with all the gripping excitement of any such tale. But his main character, Rudy, is on a mission of self-redemption because he believes that his German-American father is collaborating with the Nazis. Thus there is a study of the anguish of a persecuted personality that doubles the impact of the action on the reader. In Bound for Singapore, Pease presents a young man's romantic dreams of adventure on the sea which lead him eventually to become a seaman. The boy finds himself not bound for Singapore but an assistant oiler below decks on a dirty boat bound for New York. There is adventure, real and stark, on the sea and in New York, but not the glamorous adventure he expected to find. Still, the experience is maturing and sobering to the young man.

Real characterization takes place in most of the books, for the adventure becomes essentially a background of experience that is crucial in the life of the individual, not just a passing incident.

Recent adventure stories have a "here-and-now" quality. The modern reader does not withdraw into a realm of the shadowy past or to distant, romantically named places, quite apart from the real world. The stories have a realism about them that is refreshing. Stephen Meader, in Trap Lines North, writes with all the detailed factualness of a news reporter about the boy's running a trap line.

Fiction for the Adolescent 57

The high adventure, the fight with hunger, cold, and a dangerous job, is bolstered with reality of facts and figures. Money is an ever present concern. One does not step down to London to buy a boat. One has to scheme and plan for each improvement or addition to the trap line. The book also contains a warm family relationship of teen-agers to each other and to their mother. There is no mysticism, no magic word, but the cold hard facts of real adventure. The mountain-climbing stories have a similar sense of reality in the way they are handled.

There is stark realism in Howard Pease's The Dark Adventure, a book with a theme far different from that of any of the older stories. Johnny Steven, hitchhiking across the country, becomes an amnesia victim as the result of an accident. The story then is the story of a boy on the road, of hot rods, of hopping trains, of dope-peddlers. As Johnny fends for himself, he tries to recover his identity.

Interestingly enough, the sense of reality in adventure is one of its oldest traditions. The high adventure of Robinson Crusoe was not so much in what happened as in the remarkable ability of Defoe to convince the reader that it did happen. This he did by the minutest attention to details of daily life, to bolstering his tale with exact measurements, units of weight, precise descriptions of how the hut was built, bills of lading of what he salvaged from the ship, and the like. The high success of Edward Ellsburg lies in the same thing, and one of the distinguishing characteristics of Heinlein—that places him head and shoulders above the other writers of science fiction— is the everyday quality of his books. In his two most successful, Farmer in the Sky and Rolling Stones, he takes the reader step by step through all the mathematical considerations of space living. The detailed presentation of the problem of colonizing other planets gives an authenticity in exactly the same way that the details served Robinson Crusoe. But, more important, Heinlein never forgets the small and prosaic details of daily life that give a ring of truth to the stories. In Rolling Stones, boys living on the moon are out in the junk yard of "Dealer Dan, the Spaceship Man" looking over used space ships that they might use as jalopies. Later, they become involved in a typically adolescent scheme for making money. They buy bicycles on the moon and whip off to Mars to sell them because there is a rumor of a shortage. On Mars they find the market flooded. Details of food, of inflated prices for tourist-lodging on Mars, do much to give reality to the fantasy of the stories.

The boy of today can still have high adventure; he may sail beyond the sunset through books we give him. In many ways these books today are better than the books we prized as adventure in the past, for the qualities that lift a series of actions to the realms of literature—setting, characterization, and evaluations of human living—are increasingly present in the works of modern writers.

"The Adolescent in American Fiction" by Frederic Carpenter, English Journal, 46:313-319, September, 1957. Reprinted with the permission of the National Council of Teachers of English.

> Concluding that ". . . at his best the modern American novelist of adolescence describes the problems of our adolescent civilization. . . ," this article examines the work of J. D. Salinger, Carson McCullers, and Jessamyn West. Professor Carpenter is a research associate in English at the University of California, Berkeley. His latest book is American Literature and the Dream, 1955.

"My God, what a dark world!" said Mr. Delahanty. "I lived there for a year."

"What year?"

"The year I was thirteen. —You don't know who you are then, or what you can do. You've got to make a hundred false starts. You've got to make your mark, without knowing what your mark is. Are you a coward or a hero? How do you know without involving yourself in dangerous situations? So you walk ridge poles and visit cemeteries. . ."

—In these words the father in Cress Delahanty sums up the problems besetting all adolescents who have struggled toward maturity, and particularly those who have appeared in modern American fiction. "Walking ridge poles and visiting cemeteries," Huck Finn and Tom Sawyer first brought this dark world to the attention of American readers. And in the last decade heroes as different as Holden Caulfied in The Catcher in the Rye, Mick Kelly in The Heart Is a Lonely Hunter, and Cress Delahanty, who adopted "craziness" as her trade-mark, have multiplied.

Some American critics have bewailed the fact that many of our best novels have been "children's books." They have assumed that these books have reflected the immaturity of our American society. They have pointed out that Mark Twain, the eternal "youth," gained fame by describing the boyish adventures of Tom Sawyer; and that Booth Tarkington became a best seller by poking fun at the pranks of Penrod and Sam. In the words of Huck Finn, these novels describing the escapades of childhood and adolescence have seemed to the critics "all mixed up and splendid"—that is to say, immature. If all our novels of adolescence were merely "mixed up," these critics would be right. But books about immaturity need not be immature, and a few American novels about adolescence have embodied some of the most adult wisdom that America has produced. After Tom Sawyer, Mark Twain described the growth of Huck Finn toward maturity. And after Mark Twain, other Americans have written mature novels about children and adolescents.

If we enquire further why some of these "adolescent" novels have remained merely childish and amusing, while others have become genuinely mature and wise, we come upon a paradox. The stories about adolescence which have remained merely childish have been those which have described their heroes from the superior point of view of the adult, condescendingly. The adventures of the romantic Tom Sawyer, and of Penrod and Sam, have seemed somewhat ridiculous because they have been motivated by those confusions of adolescence which their adult authors and readers have, of course, outgrown. But the novels which have achieved genuine maturity, and sometimes greatness, are those which have entered into the confusions of their adolescents at first hand, and have described them through the eyes of their protagonists. Sometimes these mature authors have told their stories in the first person, as in Huck Finn and The Catcher in the Rye, and sometimes in the third; but always the authors have remained objective, respecting their youthful heroes as human individuals and recognizing their problems as real. Indeed, these adolescent problems have often reflected the problems of their parents and elders, as in a distorting mirror.

For this reason some of these novels describing the confusions of adolescence may prove to be the most important fiction produced by our society, whose values are similarly confused. Before the Civil War, Huck Finn vacillated between a traditional loyalty to a slave-holding society and a deeply felt loyalty to the humanity of

Fiction for the Adolescent

"Nigger Jim." More recently Holden Caulfield struggled to reconcile the predatory sexual mores of his athletic and intellectual heroes with his own deeply-felt love for his young sister Phoebe and their family. And Mick Kelly instinctively sympathized with the tormented labor agitator and the disturbed deaf-mute who opposed race prejudice in her Southern town, and sought to understand their defeat.

In the following pages we shall consider the novels of J. D. Salinger, Carson McCullers, and Jessamyn West in some detail, and compare them with other lesser novels, which have either described adolescence more superficially, like Booth Tarkington's, or have treated it as a mere aspect of some larger problem, like Richard Wright's Black Boy.

It would be hard to imagine novels more different than The Catcher in the Rye, The Heart Is a Lonely Hunter, and Cress Delahanty. The first concentrates on three days in the life of an upper-class New York City boy, who has just been expelled from a private school. The second describes the various racial and social tensions of a Southern town, as seen through the eyes of the young daughter of a poor family over the period of a year. The third etches separate scenes in the life of a middle-class California girl, over a period of four years. Yet all three observe their adolescent protagonists without sentimentality, and without condescension, but with a deeply sympathetic understanding. And the problems of the three never remain merely those of adolescence, but become those of American society as well.

J. D. Salinger

Like Huck Finn, The Catcher in the Rye is narrated in the first person, and in the vernacular, by a boy who is badly "mixed up." But both Huck and Holden are intellectually honest, and both succeed in communicating their confusion and in suggesting some of the reasons for it. Both are ambivalent, and even flaunt their confusion—Huck by praising Tom Sawyer's plans as "mixed up and splendid," and Holden by defiantly wearing his red hunting cap backwards through New York City. In the end Huck plans to "light out for the territory," and Holden thinks of fleeing West, but is dissuaded by his attachment to his family, and is sent to a psychiatrist instead.

Of course the two novels differ as much as they resemble each other, and do not mean to suggest that The Catcher... is a rival of Huck Finn. Where Huck was the typical American democrat, Holden is a snob who criticizes his friends for the shabby suitcases they carry. Where Huck lived in the rich heartland of America, Holden is the product of an exclusive New York City. Salinger himself seems almost the typical New Yorker, and his short stories emphasize the emotional starvation and brittleness of the city life, which his novel only suggests. Yet his New York and its problems are perhaps as central to modern America as Mark Twain's Mississippi River was to the pioneer nineteenth century.

The quality which makes Huck Finn and Holden Caulfield brothers under the skin—and which runs through all the best of these novels—is a common hatred of hypocrisy and a search for integrity. And this emerges in spite of—or perhaps as a reaction against—the love of play-acting which is a natural and inevitable aspect of all adolescence. Just as Huck plays along with Tom's mixed up schemes, and observes the deceptions of the Duke and the Dauphin with reluctant admiration, so Holden ironically admires the amatory techniques of his roommate Stradlater who speaks in "this sincere voice," and himself makes up absurd phantasies for the mother of a classmate whom he meets on the train. Yet Holden's chief contempt is for "all those phonies," and his admiration goes out to the genuine sincerity of the two nuns he meets, and of his sister Phoebe.

Perhaps the central theme of these novels of adolescence is the individual's search for genuine values. At the end Phoebe typically corrects her brother's misquotation of the poem:

—"If a body catch a body comin' through the rye"
—"'It's 'if a body meet a body...' "

In the confused rye fields of life the worldly characters seek to "catch" people, and in revulsion Holden imagines "catching" all innocent children to protect them from destruction. "I know it's crazy," admits Holden, who suffers a nervous breakdown at the end. And similarly Huck Finn ended by exclaiming: "I can't stand it. I been there before." In their confusion, these heroes desperately seek truth.

But the ambivalence of adolescence, which runs after experience yet fears it, and admires the mixed up and splendid world while still idealizing innocence, merely reflects the similar ambivalence of American society. And here The Catcher... goes beyond Huck Finn—partly in that it describes an older boy who confronts the larger problems of sex which Huck Finn never faced, and partly in that it describes an America which also has reached "an end to innocence." Where Huck had been able to escape "civilization and its discontents" by "lighting out for the territory," now Holden must consult a psychiatrist and face those problems of growing up which our maturing society must also face.

From another perspective these same problems are described with even greater clarity and poignancy in Salinger's short story, "For Esmé—with Love and Squalor." This time the narrator is a mature American soldier, who meets an adolescent English Esmé during World War II. The clear-eyed British girl, whose father has been killed in the war, asks the American if he writes stories about "squalor" as well as "love," because she recognizes that her genteel upbringing has shielded her from experience of the dark side of life. The second half of the story then describes the chaos of the invasion of Europe, from which the narrator is saved, psychologically, by remembering the "love" of the young English Esmé. Where The Catcher... described only the confusions of innocence facing the evils of experience, "Esmé" now suggests the possible resolution of this conflict, through a recognition and acceptance of apparently "evil" experiences. The mature individual must experience and accept "squalor" as well as "love," and not try to "catch" those innocents who rush confusedly towards the experience of what may seem evil.

Carson McCullers

With greater complexity and greater realism, although perhaps with less art, Carson McCullers embodies these same problems of adolescence, and its confrontation of the evils of experience, in her novels The Heart Is a Lonely Hunter and The Member of the Wedding. The latter more resembles The Catcher in the Rye, in that it focuses on the failure of the adolescent to adjust to the confusions of the adult world. But The Heart. . . is a larger and richer book. The Member of the Wedding reached a large audience through its appearances, first as a play, and then as a moving picture. And its disturbed adolescent, Frankie Addams, embodies in exaggerated form all those traits of immaturity which other novels have described more normally, and thereby rivets our attention on them the more firmly. Frankie's feeling of desperate isolation and alienation drives her to identify herself with her older brother and his fiancée, until she tries to join them even on their honeymoon. But this grotesque situation merely emphasizes the confusion of all adolescents, and of all maladjusted members of human society.

What raises The Member of the Wedding above the merely grotesque (as described in the author's other novel Reflections in a Golden Eye) is its inclusion of other characters suggesting the parallel tragedies of other alienated people. Berenice Sadie Brown, the Negro mammy whose husband has died leaving her lonely, and her foster-brother "Honey," who runs afoul of the law, suggest the tragedy of Negroes who can never become full "members" of society; the young John Henry is the "gentle boy" who is too good for this world; while over all hangs the cloud of the atom bomb, which everyone discusses casually.

By contrast, The Heart Is a Lonely Hunter seems hardly to describe adolescence at all. The youthful Mick Kelly appears a background figure, observing and partly sharing the tragedies of the deafmutes, the Negroes, and the labor agitators. The long novel begins with the story of the two mutes and ends with the musings of Biff Brannon, who runs the "New York Café," where the rest all meet and talk. But essentially it describes the struggle of all these lonely people to come to terms with their world, to become members of their society, to find human love—in short, to become mature.

Certainly the most unusual characters in this novel are the two deaf-mutes, Singer and Antonapoulos, whose devotion to each other recalls the desperate attachment of the two lonely ranch hands in Steinbeck's Of Mice and Men. But because these are mutes, they are the more hopelessly shut off from their world, and Antonapoulos gradually regresses into insanity. But Singer (whose name is both ironic and symbolic) grows, and strangely attracts all those alienated members of society who seek human love, by his Christ-like serenity and unselfishness. Renting a room in Mick's father's house, he becomes her confidant. Bringing the labor agitator home to sleep off a drunk, he becomes the sympathetic "listener" to his impassioned pleadings. Treating the Negro doctor as his equal, he shares his tortured protests against racial inequality. But at the end when his beloved Antonapoulos dies in an asylum, he commits suicide. And this failure of love—this self-destruction of their symbol of human maturity—affects all the other characters tragically.

At the end of the novel an older Mick Kelly is left alone facing an unfriendly world. Her children's party has ended in a near riot. A free-for-all at the circus has resulted in the death of a Negro and has forced the labor agitator to leave town. Poverty now compels her to give up her dreams of a musical career, and to accept a clerk's job at Woolworth's. Biff Brannon observes her at her cafe table sympathetically but sadly. The voice of Hitler screams over the radio. —"What good was it? That was the question she would like to know. What the hell good was it?" The novel ends on this note of frustration.

Jessamyn West

In outcome and in mood, The Heart Is a Lonely Hunter and Cross (sic) Delahanty are opposite, yet the two represent different faces of the same coin. Cress is merely Mick Kelly or Frankie Addams in happier surroundings, and Cress's story describes the achievement of love where Mick's described the failure of love. Both heroines attain maturity, though in different ways. —If the story of a tragedy is necessarily greater than the story of happiness, then The Heart. . . is the better book: it follows the tradition of Hawthorne and Melville, where Cress follows the tradition of Emerson and Whitman. But to tell the story of a normal and successful heroine effectively may be more difficult, and represent a greater achievement, than to tell a tragic story. Cress is the typical adolescent American girl, and Jessamyn West has achieved the rare distinction of portraying her normal, middle-class American characters with complete success.

The quality which distinguishes Cress Delahanty, as well as Jessamyn West's other adolescent protagonists in The Friendly Persuasion, is the same which Huck Finn and The Catcher valued most—that of sincerity or integrity. Like them Cress is confused, and struggles to find out who she is. She first appears reciting romantic poetry and posturing before her mirror. Then she does "crazy" things consciously, like carrying her shoes to the school bus "to save time," and lacing them up there. Later she derives strange satisfaction from acting out grotesque "caricatures in motion" before a town audience, although nobody else appreciates them. But through all this she is consciously experimenting and attempting to make contacts with the adult world, so that unlike Holden Caulfield, she does not feel guilty in her play-acting, and unlike Huck and Holden, she never despairs of adult "civilization." When, against the advice of her closest friends, she visits an older man on his sick bed, and in the presence of his wife blurts out that she loves him, her utter sincerity makes her adolescent act so acceptable that her "love" is neither ridiculed nor rejected, but recognized for what it is—an immature but genuine fragment of all human love.

Meanwhile Cress, like all other adolescents, observes and confronts evil in its various forms. Visiting her beautiful music teacher for the night, she learns by accident of her infidelity, yet also learns that the husband loves his wife in spite of it. Visiting a classmate and her father in the poor section of town, she is horrified by his handling of snakes and torturing of them. Reading with her friend Edwin in an arroyo, the two are threatened by a bully, but Edwin breaks off a cactus with his bare hands to use as a weapon. And at the end she recognizes and accepts her grandfather's death as a kind of completion and fulfilment of life.

Fiction for the Adolescent

Like Cress Delahanty, all Jessamyn West's characters are normal, healthy, middle-class Americans—but with this difference. What gives them warmth and integrity, and ultimately importance, is their inheritance and shared realization of a traditional American idealism often lost in the wasteland of our twentieth century. Cress achieves fulfilment where Mick Kelly remains frustrated, partly because Cress and her creator belong to the tradition of self-realization inherited from Emerson and Whitman. And in The Friendly Persuasion, the adolescent children of a Quaker family meet the challenge of war and its devastation face to face.

Josh Birdwell, the son of a Quaker minister, must decide between his inherited faith and an active participation in the Civil War. And this ideal conflict raises him far above the normal adolescent facing the usual problems of growing up. He becomes the typical American idealist, facing the end of national innocence, and makes his mature decision to participate with his countrymen in the evil of this world. And this theme is central. Unlike Mark Twain and his nineteenth century hero, the modern adolescent cannot simply escape to the West, but must face the evils of civilization wherever he finds them. His problem is the problem of all of us.

Against this background the adolescent adventure of Penrod and Sam appear merely trivial. And in Seventeen, Booth Tarkington's superior sarcasm becomes almost coy: "Seventeen sometimes finds it embarrassing to walk two hundred feet, or thereabouts, toward a group of people who steadfastly watch the long approach." Similarly, Herman Wouk's recent novel, The City Boy, describes the misadventures of his young hero, Herman Bookbinder, mostly for the laughs. The mature elders of Penrod and Sam, and of Herman, know all the answers, of course. And therefore they find these callow adolescents simply amusing. When their characters grow up, they will see the world for what it is—a clear pattern of black and white, where all their childish confusions will disappear. And in this world of literary entertainment, all serious problems simply vanish.

At the opposite extreme, some modern writers describe life as a hopeless problem, to which adolescence furnishes the hopeless prologue. Particularly the Negro novelists Richard Wright and Ralph

Ellison see nothing but blackness in a bitter world. In Black Boy Wright has written the autobiography of the adolescent Southern Negro. And on a higher level, Ralph Ellison has suggested symbolically the hopeless confusion of values faced by the young Negro, in Invisible Man. Here the old American idealism has produced only "The Golden Day Saloon," and a modern "Mr. Emerson" runs a paint factory whose motto is: "Keep America Pure with Liberty Paints."—If the adolescent boy is an "invisible" black, he faces a seemingly insoluble problem in his struggle to find out his mature identity.

But these two extremes merely define the frame of reference within which the modern American novelist of adolescence must work. Besides those mentioned, many other novelists have treated the theme. Steinbeck's stories of the Red Pony are in some ways the most perfect of all, but are in miniature. Thomas Wolfe's Look Homeward, Angel describes vividly the problems of an American adolescent, but on a gigantic scale. Tea and Sympathy, like The Member of the Wedding, focuses on a single phase of the subject. And there are many more. But at his best the modern American novelist of adolescence describes the problems of his protagonists so that they become also the problems of our adolescent civilization, with both its mixed-up confusion and its splendid potentiality.

"How Do I Love Thee?" by Margaret A. Edwards.[1]
The English Journal, 41:335-340, September, 1952.
Reprinted with the permission of the National Council
of Teachers of English.

If one were to play the game "associations" with a group of girls in their teens and called out the word "love, " it is quite likely that the youngest would think "boy-friend" while the older would think "lover" or "marriage"; for love does not mean the same thing to a high school freshman as it does to the "smoothie" who leads the senior prom. And so, when a high school girl asks the librarian to help her select love stories, the librarian first estimates the emotional maturity of the girl, then searches for a book that tells of love in language the girl can understand. She suggests love stories very much as physicians prescribe sulfa drugs, by familiarizing herself with old and new products in the field, by prescribing as best she can, and by keeping a sharp lookout for reactions.

The Boy-Friend

When the girl of twelve or thirteen years of age discovers that "it's love that makes the world go round, " she is both dismayed and delighted to think that soon she may be identified with this strange force that keeps the world revolving. But love to her is a mystery. About all she is sure of in the beginning is that girlfriends[2] are not enough. As fourteen-year-old Anne Frank said in her diary, "I'm glad after all that the Van Daans have a son, and not a daughter; my conquest could never have been so difficult, so beautiful, so good, if I had not happened to hit on someone of the opposite sex. "

Girls in their early teens are not concerned with eternal triangles nor with the anguish and ecstasy of love. They want to know how a first date is made; how to be one of the crowd that go around in couples; what a boy and girl can possibly find to talk about for an entire evening; how kissing fits into the picture; and the advisability of going steady. Yet it is only since 1942 that librarians have been able to satisfy this need. With the publication of Seventeenth Summer, the awakening of love was first depicted for teenagers in language they could understand. Since then, young love has been written about over and over to the delight of the young girl whose more critical elders wonder whether she should not be reading the classics. Of course she should read the classics, too; but at her age nothing is more important than a feeling of social security (not the government kind), and the best of these teen-age stories, slight as they are, give her understanding of her peers and of herself and help smooth the road to happiness. They also develop a genuine love of reading which remains long after the girl outgrows this interest in stories of first love.

Maureen Daly is unique. It is interesting that she has stood behind Seventeenth Summer as her testament to youth and has not converted her enorous popularity into specie of the realm. It is interesting that a generation of bobby-soxers despaired of by the moralists have identified themselves with unsophisticated Angie Morrow. It is interesting that in sixteen years no other story of first love has rivaled Seventeenth Summer in quality or popularity. The nearest contemporary rival in popularity is probably the author who writes under two names, Cavanna and Headley. Going on Sixteen and A Date for Dianne have much to say to shy girls who must learn that the road to self-assurance and popularity is paved with thoughts and deeds that center around other people rather than one's self. And in her stories this author says these things in a style that is entertaining and persuasive.

The nearest rival in quality is probably Mary Stolz. In both To Tell Your Love and The Sea Gulls Woke Me she draws sharp characterizations, brings poignancy to the problems of youth, and has well-developed plots. And yet, while her stories are enjoyed, girls in Baltimore who read them do not send their friends to the library with the general understanding that their lives will not be worth living until they read these books. It may be that this author has limited her audience by writing a junior novel so mature in its concepts that it is best understood by college girls who choose their

Fiction for the Adolescent 71

reading from lists of great books or best sellers and do not read junior novels, however good they may be. In <u>The Sea Gulls Woke Me</u> Mrs. Stolz includes brief discussions of T. S. Eliot and Macaulay; she skilfully depicts the hopeless fascination that an "arty" author, an older man, has for a young college girl, thereby giving her story a very grown-up tone, which many girls read with pleasure and profit but not too often with a deep enough understanding, because they are unacquainted with some of her characters or have not come across some of her situations in their limited experiences. So while librarians and book reviewers compare Stolz with Maureen Daly, the young people themselves do not.

Despite all this theorizing about limiting one's audience, there is no recipe for writing for young people; for, as soon as we decide that Mary Stolz seems to have overshot her mark, we think of <u>Junior Miss</u>, a sophisticated sketch of first love aimed at adults who read the <u>New Yorker</u>, which hit the bull's-eye with teen-agers.

Among the stories of early love, several authors have had the interest and skill to show girls, in an entertaining story, the difference between solid gold and glittering brass in boy-friends. Bitsy Close of <u>Stand Fast and Reply</u> by Lavinia Davis; Liz Ericson of <u>Take Care of My Little Girl</u> by Peggy Goodin; Thankful Curtis of <u>Bright Island</u> by Mabel Robinson; and Mary Clayborne of <u>Big Doc's Girl</u> by Medearis all learned, as do their readers, that shiny cars, fur coats, social aplomb, and a thirst for fame cannot in the end compete successfully with character, kindness of heart, and ability.

Many other stories of first love might be mentioned here, but two titles must be included—one very new and one very old. <u>Anne Frank: The Diary of a Young Girl</u> has as its subtitle "An Extraordinary Document of Adolescence." When the Nazis occupied Holland and began hunting down Jews, thirteen-year-old Anne with her family, the Van Daan family and their son Peter, and a Mr. Dussel hid for two years in the abandoned half of an old office building in Amsterdam, never leaving it for two years until they were discovered at last and taken to a concentration camp where Anne died. Her poignant diary, found on the floor of the rifled apartment, is extraordinary for many reasons but is cited here as an exquisite study of a young girl's heart opening to love. It should be equally moving to both adults and adolescents.

Finally, we come to Jane Eyre, the story of first love that stands by itself. This long old novel does not help young girls to gain a sense of security; its language is out of date and it sometimes borders on melodrama; but it gets there just the same. It is read and loved by girls of all ages. Its author, the old maid from Haworth parsonage, is Maureen Daly's most dangerous challenger.

Love and Marriage

The transition from boy-friend to lover is gradual and probably can be made most easily in books by reading love stories in a family setting. Three delightful stories of young girls whose families are involved in their social life are Elizabeth Gray's Fair Adventure, Anne Ritner's The Green Bough, and Leonora Weber's enjoyable series beginning with Meet the Malones. Then there is the more adult family novel with love as a theme. Rose Wilder Lane's Let the Hurricane Roar is a book to be cherished. It is a fine story of the early West, it tells of courage and character, and, for the purpose of this discussion, it is a compelling and convincing picture of true love without a false or sentimental note. Even though the central characters are married in the very beginning of the story, it is generally beloved.

When a girl comes to the library with a theater program in her hand, when she tells of reading her mother's book-club books or asks about a best seller, or when some senior boy asks her to his prom, she is probably ready to read adult novels where lovers take the place of boy-friends and love and marriage are more interesting in stories than going steady or being one of the crowd. When in doubt on such an occasion, we reach for Agnes Turnbull. Either The Rolling Years or Gown of Glory will do nicely. Certainly Agnes Turnbull is not a finished stylist, nor are her novels profound; yet they have a tremendous appeal and unquestionably afford girls vicarious experience. Girls who read The Rolling Years seem to say to themselves, "This is what it is like to be loved, to marry, to have children, and to grow old." Years ago, many of us had the same

Fiction for the Adolescent 73

feeling when we read Tennyson's Ulysses and heard the hero say, "I have drunk life to the lees."

Once when John Erskine was lecturing to a class on Walt Whitman, he said, "Whitman was interested in the fertility of the earth, in birth and death, in the children coming home for Thanksgiving and the simple joys and sorrows of living, and if you are not interested in these things too, it might be well to ask yourself why." Agnes Turnbull is not the artist Walt Whitman was, but she is interested in the same simple, basic, important things; and, though she is speaking to adults, young people who listen in can understand. In The Gown of Glory she lends dignity to the simple life and charm to everyday events in a small town. She writes of goodness, grief, sin, family life, a rose in a young girl's hair, and life as it is attainable by the average person. As the young girl loves Maureen Daly for showing her what it is like to grow up, so the older girl loves Agnes Turnbull for letting her understand something of love and marriage.

Another author who tells of love in a manner equally agreeable to adults and teen-agers is Nevil Shute. His technical firsthand knowledge of aviation and his sensitive understanding of women make him equally popular with boys and girls. His love stories have a nice tingle, they are well written, and they usually present a good picture of another country with people who react as do their brothers over the world.

Winter Wheat by Mildred Walker is a fine story of a lost love that shows how one lives on with a broken heart until life offers a different kind of happiness to which the dormant heart must respond as winter wheat to the sun and rain.

Three good pictures of marriage are to be found in O'Hara's My Friend Flicka, Freedman's Mrs. Mike, and Buck's East Wind, West Wind. Though My Friend Flicka is usually thought of as a horse story, it is really the story of a boy and of his parents, Nell and Rob McLaughlin, who differ about the affairs of the Goosebar Ranch and about the rearing of their sons; who storm at each other and at times consider giving their marriage up; but who, in the end, make allowances for each other and ride out the storms, because they are truly in love. In Freedman's Mrs. Mike Mary Catherine learns that the love of a man can enable a woman to triumph over loneliness, isolation, hardship, and grief; and that if one truly loves and is loved in return, nothing else matters, for no fulfilment equals that of a good marriage. East Wind, West Wind tells of a Chinese girl married to a strange man whom she comes to love so much that she gives up all the things once near and dear to her to win his love, and by doing this she finds happiness and love. In none of the three novels is marriage a matter of living happily ever afterward but rather a story of two people learning to adjust to each other and, in the process, discovering that love is more important than keeping one's individuality intact.

Adolescents read Pride and Prejudice and Wuthering Heights with enjoyment, though they usually prefer the sweetness and light of Jane Eyre to the gloom and force of Wuthering Heights. They like A Tale of Two Cities, but few of them will read Dickens' other novels. The delightful style of Dodie Smith's I Capture the Castle has great appeal for the discriminating older girl, but the matter-of-fact unimaginative adolescent is dismayed when she opens the book to read, "I write this sitting in the kitchen sink. That is, my feet are in it; the rest of me is on the draining-board, which I have padded with our dog's blanket and the tea-cosy." Both boys and girls thoroughly enjoy The Caine Mutiny. Here is adventure, humor, love, realism, a good plot, and a breezy style. A more moving, more mature novel of love and the sea is Monsarrat's The Cruel Sea. The men of the Compass Rose ranged from inexperienced Baker to promiscuous Evans to unsteady Ferraby, well-bred Morell, and lovable Lockhart; and so their love for women ranged from animality to ardor, from crudity to tenderness.

Some of our leading psychiatrists and other advanced thinkers hold that Americans, with their incurably romantic ideas of love, do their young people a disservice when they lead them to believe that love is a rosy cloud on which one floats through life; that after one falls in love, he marries and lives happily ever after because love conquers all. These thinkers hold that when storms strike the good ship "Matrimony," young people brought up on starry-eyed love are

Fiction for the Adolescent 75

all too often overwhelmed by the flood, because they are totally unprepared for the seamy side of love or for the heartache and suffering that often accompany it. If this theory is correct, books like The Cruel Sea can afford young people a foretaste of love in many of its various manifestations as they read of the uneventful peace it brought Ericson, the sense of stability it gave Ferraby, the excruciating suffering it was to Morell, and the beauty and pain it combined for Lockhart.

Two books not rightly stories but popular for their themes of love are Rostand's Cyrano de Bergerac and Husted's Love Poems of Six Centuries. The latter is one of the very few volumes of poetry in demand by young people in the various communities of Baltimore. Two recent books that temper love with humor in a manner likely to appeal to young people are Max Shulman's The Many Loves of Dobie Gillis and Neill Wilson's The Nine Brides and Granny Hite.

Many critics look with contempt on the majority of historical novels. Certainly too many have been written with lurid jackets and sensational plots, but there are also many fine historical novels that are not only entertaining love stories but give a true picture of a past that made the present—of peasants and kings and the whole pageant of history; and because this is done in story form with emotional content, it often leaves a more lasting feeling for history than the most carefully prepared textbooks. Among the worth-while historical novels popular with teen-agers who like love and history combined are: Guthrie, The Way West; Costain, The Black Rose; Shellabarger, The Prince of Foxes and The Captain from Castile; McNeilly, Each Bright River; Wellman, The Iron Mistress; Barnes, My Lady of Cleves; Mitchell, Gone with the Wind; Stone, Immortal Wife and The President's Lady; Thane's Williamsburg series; and those two veterans—Johnston, To Have and To Hold, and Orczy, The Scarlet Pimpernel.

As we said above, one cannot always predict the appeal a love story will have for teen-agers. Often books that librarians and teachers and professional critics like leave young people cold. In Baltimore we thought Macken's Rain on the Wind was a real find for our better readers; but so far the enthusiasm expressed is the librarian's. Edmonds' Wedding Journey seems to us to have a very special charm, but it sits on the shelf a great deal of the time. Ullman strikes few sparks; Rumer Godden is too subtle; and Dickens, as was said above, too slow. Willa Cather, with her noble themes and polished style, is too mature for the general run of teen-agers in Baltimore.

How few young people, or adults for that matter, can appreciate a book for the style of its writing! This is always disappointing to the adult who expects more results from his efforts to lead young people to appreciate beauty of expression. But style is a very mature concept and almost all of us fail to appreciate it in some one of the arts. We listen with a dull ear to Shostakovich; we look at the paintings of the modern artists with lack-luster eyes; we cannot name three modern sculptors, or we think ballet trivial. Consequently, many young people do not understand why words set down by Willa Cather are literature, and it is very difficult to show them why.

As beauty is its own excuse for being, the pleasure a good book gives young people is excuse enough for including it in a young people's collection; but, when a love story goes beyond entertainment to point up a problem or bring the past to life or convince us that all men are brothers, it is doubly welcome on our shelves. Such love stories as Quality by Sumner or Earth and High Heaven by Graham make a telling plea for tolerance by showing us, without a sermon, how innocent people may suffer when they might so easily be happy if prejudice were banished. In these days when young people must learn quickly of the brotherhood of man, we appreciate those love stories whose characters are the people of other countries. Loomis' And Ride Forth Singing makes a French girl's choice between two suitors a problem any American girl might face. Nevil Shute's The Legacy is such an appealing picture of Australia and its people that it must at least have convinced the author—he has moved there to live. His Chequer Board enlists the reader's sympathy for the Siamese, the English, and the American Negro. Stinetorf's White Witch Doctor is a romance with an African setting, and Peal Buck's novels of love, set in China, have gone far to make the Chinese pop-

Fiction for the Adolescent 77

ular with the American people. Though we have been fighting the Chinese for two years, little hatred can be engendered against them. Though there are various reasons for this, novels portraying the virtues and charm of the Chinese may have played a part. From the age of King Solomon wise people have realized that wisdom doubles in value if understanding accompanies it. Love stories if well written enlarge the understanding of young people and add to their emotional growth. With some counsel from adults familiar with the field a girl in early adolescence can progress from Seventeenth Summer to The Rolling Years and East Wind, West Wind and then be ready as she emerges from the teens to learn of Kristin Lavransdatter, Héloise and Abélard, Anna Karenina, and other immortals who once counted the world well lost for love.

Notes

1. Then Co-ordinator of Work with Young People, Enoch Pratt Free Library, Baltimore, Maryland.
2. I think this word must explain the origin of "boy-friend," a term I apologize for using, but what else can this awkward fourteen-year-old boy be called? He is not a beau in this atomic age; he is too coltish to be called an admirer; and, fortunately, he isn't a lover.

Part Three. Non-Fiction for the Adolescent

"Biographies for Teen-Agers" by Learned T. Bulman. The English Journal, 47:487-494, November, 1958. Reprinted with the permission of the National Council of Teachers of English.

Despite the fact that the biographies discussed in this article are aimed at the younger reader, I have more than once found myself so engrossed in the book at hand that midnight has long passed without my knowledge. Everyone of them had something to teach me, and many of them are loaded with factual data that had managed to escape me in a reasonably voracious reading life. If they can do this for me, why not for the teen-ager?

It should be emphasized at this time that many of these works are the narrative or story form often called fictionalized biography. No doubt this has annoyed some English teachers, but one must ask himself what one expects the student to get from reading a biography. If you are seeking great works of literature—even juvenile literature—this is the area in which you are least likely to find them. Few, if any, would fall into the classic status. Only occasionally is there a bright star who would be considered a juvenile Harold Lamb, Emil Ludwig, or Hesketh Pearson. What then is the value of these pattern pieces?

It has been my impression that biographies are frequently assigned with the idea of encouraging the student to make something of himself (?) through the vicarious experience of reading about one who has succeeded. They are also assigned to let the youngster view the whole person (whoever he may be), not just the popular or historical memory of him. To succeed in either of these aims, as far as the middling reader is concerned, there are certain requisites. The author must have presented his facts entertainingly or at least succeeded in sustaining interest. He must not philosophize too much into the why of the subject. And usually he must have accomplished all this in 300 pages or less.

The subject is not as important, if the librarian or teacher is a good salesman. Mary Ann Bickerdyke or Joseph Pulitzer—though not well known to this age—will be eagerly read if properly introduced.

It should be understood that this paper is written from the viewpoint of a public librarian. For that very reason, it is mandatory that the rather different attitude such a person assumes when asked for a biography by a student be clarified. The public librarian is seldom acquainted with the individual's I.Q., reading score, or other pedagogical measurements. He is equally unaware of how well the student does, or better, approaches his school work. This does not for a moment imply that he does not know personally the many students who come to him, and recognize their seeming potential. Again, the problem is not the student who will come in and ask for Sandburg or someone similar suggested by the teacher. The problem students are those who can read better and are not doing so, and those who can just about read.

For those who can just read, but have somehow reached junior or senior high school, books by Ronald Syme, Clara Judson, or even some of the Landmark and World Landmark titles might help. As good as we think the latter are for informing the fourth, fifth, and sixth graders about United States and world historical events and leaders, we do not as a rule recommend them to the older students. However, some of these Random House titles that may be the answer for the slow readers are Sterling North's Abe Lincoln and George Washington, Vincent Sheean's Thomas Jefferson, John Gunther's Alexander the Great, and Emily Hahn's Leonardo da Vinci. The majority of the books that will be discussed in this paper will be aimed at the neither good nor bad, but just middling reader.

After this possibly long-winded, but necessary, introduction to the author's status and attitudes, it is best to push immediately into the subject at hand—namely biographies written for teen-agers. Our main concern will be the publishers' dream designation of "12 to 16," on occasion, "14-up," which so often of recent years has appeared on the inside flap of the dust cover of these books.

The firm of Julian Messner, Inc., is head and shoulders above

Non-Fiction for the Adolescent

all other publishing houses in this field. Their Shelf of Biographies has in its (forgive the expression) stable of authors, some really good writers. One out of three of the better biographies would seem to be published by Messner, although there are no figures to substantiate such a statement. Other houses have one or two people who consistently turn out good material, but with these exceptions, the biographies that have excited our interest have been non-series items. Books no longer in print have been avoided. That your library may have them is fine, but why frustrate those teaching in new schools, whose libraries, equally new, cannot obtain such material?

Four Prolific Writers

We will first consider the more prolific writers. In this category are: Jeannette Covert Nolan, Jeannette Eaton, Shannon Garst, and Marguerite Vance. Although no two necessarily follow the same pattern, all four of them use the narrative approach to a greater or lesser degree and all are formula writers. Of the four, the two Jeannettes, Eaton and Nolan, are the best literary artists.

Much of what is said about Nolan is equally true of Eaton. There is such similarity of approach that some of their works could have been done by either. They have both written top-notch items as well as one or two that aren't quite as interesting. They, as will be true of most of our authors, deal in blacks and whites. Their subjects are either good or bad; there is little or no attempt at gradation.

Jeannette Covert Nolan is a Messner author. She usually averages 180 to 190 pages per book, always has a bibliography, and usually has an index. She has written about Abraham Lincoln, Andrew Jackson, Benedict Arnold, Clara Barton, Florence Nightingale, Eugene Field, George Rogers Clark, O. Henry, John Brown, and La Salle. A few of her books are geared to the average ten to fourteen-year-old reader; the rest are for the twelve to sixteen age. They seem to be well researched, are well written, very readable, and add flesh and blood to what occasionally could be a skeletal subject.

Jeannette Eaton has used a number of publishers. She does not always have bibliographies and indexes. She averages 250 pages, although her Trumpeter's Tale (Louis Armstrong) is 191 and Leader by Destiny (George Washington) is 402. She also is a good researcher and reporter and has several items that are for a little older audience than those of Nolan. Other of her books still in print are David Livingston; Gandhi; Lone Journey (Roger Williams); Narcissa Whitman; Eleanor Roosevelt; and Young Lafayette.

Shannon Garst is a western devotee. All of her work is devoted to mountain men, Indians, scouts, and legendary figures of the West and Southwest. Her research is good. The vocabulary and style (which is choppier than in most books we will discuss) recommend her for those restless readers who will find that many of her subjects would make good television heroes—or already have. Wild Bill Hickock, James Bowie, Kit Carson, and Crazy Horse are samples of such figures. On the other hand, not all of her subjects are as well known outside of their home grounds as are most of the people covered by other authors for this age. Other of her books feature Big-foot Wallace (of the Texas Rangers), Chief Joseph of the Nez Perces, Jim Bridger, Joe Meek, Custer, Buffalo Bill, Sitting Bull, and William Bent.

Marguerite Vance is a romanticist. All of her biographies concern women who either have been great themselves, or have helped their men to become so. There is a story-book quality, an almost preciousness, that will appeal to the teen-age girls who enjoy historial fiction, but this does not detract from evident care for factual writing. She is our "thinnest" author, more often reaching 160 pages than 180. There is never a bibliography or an index. All of these facts make her particularly inviting to the non-reading girl who has to read a biography, but is afraid of getting a book which looks like one. To date Vance has written for Dutton: Empress Josephine; On Wings of Fire (Nathaniel Hawthorne's daughter, Rose, who became Mother Alphonsa); Elizabeth Tudor; Jacksons of Tennessee; Lady Jane Grey; Marie Antoinette; Lees of Arlington; Martha, Daughter of Virginia (Washington); and Flight of the Wildling (Elizabeth of Austria).

Non-Fiction for the Adolescent

Selected Biographies

Turning to less prolific authors, we come first to Rachel Baker who has written five excellent biographies which, on a rating scale, would place her almost at the top. Even more important, she has often chosen almost impossible people to write about and yet succeeded admirably. Her first and longest (248 pages) book, <u>First Woman Doctor</u> (the story of Elizabeth Blackwell, M. D.), has had many foreign editions. She next chose an even lesser known subject, William Thomas Green Morton, a pioneer in the use of ether. In 1950 her <u>Chaim Weizman</u> vividly told not only the story of Weizman, but made one aware of Israel's battle to again become a nation. Her other titles are <u>Sigmund Freud</u> and <u>Angel of Mercy</u> (Dorothea Lynde Dix). Miss Baker writes sympathetically and has the ability to become part of her subject. One sees, with Miss Dix, the inhuman conditions of the insane, and one experiences, with Dr. Blackwell, the vicissitudes of a woman pioneering in a man's field. Messner publishes Baker's books which average 180 to 224 pages with index and, where possible, bibliography.

One is often of two minds when one learns of a new biography for teen-agers. Why did the author choose that particular person to write about, and why, in some cases, wasn't it done sooner? Alvin F. Harlow, an established author, with work in many fields, brings such thoughts to mind. Why he chose Joel Chandler Harris (Uncle Remus), Henry Bergh (founder of the ASPCA), and Bret Harte is less important than that he has done a good job with them. Careful research and a good index, in all but the Harris book, make them fine items for book reports. His earlier books, the Harris, Harte, and Theodore Roosevelt, ran from 278 to 307 pages. His more recent works, which also include an Andrew Carnegie and a family work on the Ringlings of circus fame, run about 180 pages each. All six are part of the Messner Shelf.

Our next three authors have written only three or four biographies each and have very little in common. Of all the authors mentioned in this article, Alice Desmond comes the closest to adult writing and usually is marked "14 and up." There is a tremendous

84   Adolescent Literature

amount of research evident in her work. She has two things in common with Vance: She writes about women and her books lack indexes. But there any similarity ends. Her writing is more scholarly than Vance's and her books are about twice as long (275 to 300 pages). She offers a bibliography, a number of photographs and pictures, and, to date, has been published by Dodd, Mead. Four of her biographies—Alexander Hamilton's Wife; Glamorous Dolly Madison; Martha Washington; and Bewitching Betsy Bonaparte (American wife of Napoleon's brother, Jerome)—have successfully painted a picture of the dress, living conditions, politics, and general thinking of their respective times. Like most of our authors, she takes the liberty of inventing dialogue and thought for her subjects. At no time, however, does it seem forced or unlikely. This is another whose works should be equally useful to social studies as well as to English classes.

Manuel Komroff has done biographies of Julius Caesar, Mozart Marco Polo, and Napoleon. He averages 180 to 190 pages, always indexes, usually has a bibliography, and has been published by Messner and Knopf. He uses simple language in a third-person storybook style. He does not offer much shading in his characterizations; they are either good or bad, but seldom some of both. He has a short staccato sentence style that may bother some readers, and likes to repeat points he fears may be missed. For all of this, his material seems well reseached and is clearly reported.

A comparatively new name to this field is Iris Noble. Her biography of Nellie Bly appeared almost simultaneously with those by Nina Brown Baker and by Mignon Rittenhouse, but was judged superior to the others. Her next book was Joseph Pulitizer, and her most recent is Clarence Darrow. She enjoys writing about people with a mission. The first of her subjects wished to bring recognition and respect for women in the field of journalism. The next, who incidentally provided Nellie Bly her step to fame, wanted to bring all the news to his readers. Methods were unimportant as long as the true story was printed. His greatest mission was probably forcing the recognition of journalism as a respected profession demanding specialized training. The last of Miss Noble's knights has

Non-Fiction for the Adolescent

been best remembered for his penchant to champion the underdog in legal battle—particularly the one who represented a cause. His successes and failures filled many a column in his day. Miss Noble's journalistic background is evident in her work. She sometimes speaks in headlines, but never at the expense of lesser necessary information. There is a feeling of immediacy in all of these titles which average 191 pages, have index and bibliography, and are also published by Messner.

A specialist in yet a different way is Shirley Graham. Her forte is Negroes—well or lesser known for their part in the formation of our nation. Subjects for her books are Phyllis Wheatley, a little-known slave poetess of the American Revolutionary War period; Benjamin Banneker, born a freeman, who was known in the late 1700's for his knowledge of astronomy, his published almanac, and his help in laying out the city of Washington, D.C.; Frederick Douglass, escaped slave during the Civil War, who used his journalistic and oratorical skills to help free his people; Booker T. Washington; and Dr. George Washington Carver, whose biography Miss Graham co-authored with George Lipscomb.

Shirley Graham writes with a true feeling for her subjects— giving them dimension in a style that is lively and yet, when necessary, detailed. One can rejoice at each success of a character and feel, not pity, but the determination to try again after each failure. All of these books have been printed by Messner, run from 180 to 240 pages, and usually have an index and bibliography.

A book that won the 1955 Newbery award and one that was a runner up for it in 1957 are worthy of discussion here. The first is Jean Lee Latham's 251-page <u>Carry on, Mr. Bowditch</u>, published by Houghton, Mifflin. This is actually recommended for the ten to fourteen age level but is a really accomplished piece of writing. Miss Latham has succeeded in making a comparatively unknown person come alive on every page of her book. Unlike a number of the Newbery winners, which seem to be chosen by librarians more because they have a beauty of writing (usually lost on the child) than because they tell a good story and do it well, <u>Carry on, Mr. Bowditch</u> has been well received by the youngsters and may be just the book to give to the not-so-good reader who needs a book with bounce. Miss Latham's Trail Blazer of the Seas, about Matthew Maury, is not as interesting a book or subject, and her On Stage, Mr. Jefferson stops much too soon in Joseph Jefferson's life to be a really acceptable biography.

The runner-up referred to is Leo Gurko's Tom Paine, Freedom's Apostle. It is published by Thomas Crowell, has 213 pages and an index. In general format it reminds one of the Messner titles. It is written in the third person, and the writing is superior to that in most of the titles mentioned up to now. It calls a spade a spade and in no way tries to whitewash either Paine or the great men he dealt with in his lifetime. Gouverneur Morris, John Adams, even George Washington are seen as they were and not as legend has made them.

Our next concern will be with those writers who have succeeded in benefiting us with one or two items of significance. Such a person is Phyllis Wynn Jackson whose Golden Footlights pleased us so much that on a visit to San Francisco we went out of our way to learn more about that merry madcap named Lotta Crabtree. Although little known to recent generations, in her day she was second to none in the world of musical comedy. Her rise from dancing and singing as a child for miners in the rip-roaring camps of the old West to stardom on Broadway is vivid and enjoyable reading. Holiday House has printed this 310-page chapter in the history of musical comedy.

A title that has worn itself out several times on our shelves is The Great Houdini by Beryl Williams and Samuel Epstein, a husband and wife team who together and separately have written on a wide range of subjects. Nothing thrills a youngster more than a peek into the unknown, and what could be more mysterious than the secrets of a great magician and escape artist? The authors have brought the excitement of success, and enough explanation of how some of Houdini's tricks were achieved, to make every youngster who reads this pass on the good word. Bibliography and index are provided in this 182-page offering from Messner.

The constant need for first-class biographies of women is

Non-Fiction for the Adolescent   87

aided by Nina Brown Baker, a prolific writer who has directed much of her material to a younger audience. Of those intended for older readers, her books on Garibaldi, Bolivar, and Juarez are notable additions to this genre of writing. To our mind, however, her very best is Cyclone in Calico. It is the story of Mary Ann Bickerdyke—a rough, salty housewife who worked tirelessly as nurse, cook, and friend in battle hospitals of the Civil War. Not content with remaining in the larger cities, she followed the troops, knowing that often more lives were lost in those hours immediately after battle than on the battle field. An extensive bibliography and most complete index are found in this 278-page Little-Brown publication.

Long before the cry for a stronger science training was made, a number of notable scientists' lives were being tailored for the teen-age market. The author who has done the most accomplished job in this field is Elma Ehrlich Levinger. Of her three offerings, Albert Einstein is probably the most accurate and detailed. This is understandable when one remembers that Galileo and Leonardo da Vinci did not have about them reporters who could immortalize their extemporizing. Galileo is the most fictionalized, the author having fewer records to work with. Da Vinci, fortunately, left copious notebooks. All three books have index and bibliography, average 175 to 190 pages, and are printed by Messner.

Also from the Messner presses are the lives of Michael Faraday and Isaac Newton by Harry Sootin. If it is possible to give life and feeling to a biography of a scientist, Sootin has done it. This remark is made because perusal of many such books has shown that the single-mindedness of these great men has frequently caused them to lead a semi-sheltered, almost dull life.

One scientist who led anything but a dull life, despite a crippling disability that for many might have been a handicap, was Charles Proteus Steinmetz. Sigmund Lavine, whose Wandering Minstrels We is an excellent dual life of Gilbert and Sullivan, of light opera fame, has done an equally fascinating job for the genius of electricity, often called the Wizard of Schenectady. Steinmetz's active interest in civic affairs, his tremendous influence at Union College, his hobbies of cacti, orchids, and wild and domesticated animals are combined into a highly readable and entertaining volume of 241 pages, printed by Dodd, Mead.

The middling to poor male student often is unable to settle down with a biography of Gandhi, Julius Caesar, or even George Rogers Clark. Eaton's story of Louis Armstrong and even Shannon Garst's tales of Bowie and Hickok may not work. The next and too often only, answer is a sports personality. Unfortunately one cannot get excited over the caliber of the sports biographies extant. Gene Schoor, Milton Shapiro, Joe Trimble and others have manufactured lives of our sports heroes of the day, but they seldom have much to say, due no doubt to the fact that there just isn't much to write about these people. It is only the occasional Lou Gehrig by Frank Graham that succeeds in attaining some stature in this field.

Biography Series

There is one series of biographies that rates special commendation. These books do not specifically fall into the framework that has been set up for this paper but the high quality of authorship and the compactness of presentation make them of particular value to the better high school reader. The Alfred A. Knopf publishing company has, for several years, been printing the Great Lives in Brief series. Authors such as Andre Maurois, Rumer Godden, Albert Guerard, and Stewart Holbrook have succeeded in capturing in 205 or 206 pages the very being of such people as Hans Christian Andersen, Napoleon III, and Alexandre Dumas. The smallness of the books should in no way discourage English and social studies teachers from not only accepting but encouraging reports on volumes from the series. Andre Guerard's Napoleon (the First) and Ruth Moore's Charles Darwin are good examples of these masterpieces of distillation which should and often do encourage the student reader to hunt out larger and more detailed biographies of the same people.

A series of biographies that most teachers may not consider inclusive enough for book reports, but which we think particularly well done, are the art biographies by Elizabeth Ripley. She has managed to digest in seventy pages, illustrated with black and white reproductions of the better works of these masters, an almost crystal-like view of such fine painters as Van Gogh, Rembrandt, Michelangelo, Goya, da Vinci, and Ruebens. At a time when television has blessed us with Omnibus, the Leonard Bernstein lectures on music for children, and discussion of art by teachers like Meyer Schapiro, we could do worse than to recommend these thin, but informative works published by Oxford University Press.

This is by no means an exhaustive list of biographies for this age. The reader has no doubt thought of several fine individual biographies that could or should have been part of this paper. No attempt has been made to include all the fields that biography covers. Several authors who have a number of biographies were purposely omitted because they are dull.

Our purpose in writing this paper was to act as a proxy reader and reporter. It has been our observation that the average English teacher seldom has the time to read many of the books that are written purposely for the teen-ager. This, we hope, may have eased that work.

"Finding the Right Poem" by Mary V. Lamson, English Journal, 46:148-153, March, 1957. Reprinted with the permission of the National Council of Teachers of English.

> There is no frigate like a book
> To take us lands away,
> Nor any coursers like a page
> Of prancing poetry.

The problem: how to find the poetry that will prance for John, average; Susie, "brainy"; and Joe, retarded. To find for each of them poetry that will amuse, inspire, move emotionally, or interest intellectually—to find for them not only what is within their reach but also that which will help them grow beyond their present grasp.

Since it is impossible to select poetry for anyone without taking account of his interests, we may get help from considering some typical adolescent concerns. First of all, of course, is a dominant interest in "myself." For that reason many teen-agers respond emotionally to rather introspective poems which they may not fully comprehend. Tied in closely with this self-preoccupation is a natural interest in romantic love; the changing physical and psychological nature of the adolescent intensifies this interest, especially among girls from the sophomore year on.

Another teen-age trademark is an interest in humor, in almost any vein—Holmes, Service, Daly, Guiterman, Nash, "anything for a laugh" as they often say, and this factor often provides a springboard to the cultivation of an appreciation of poetry when all else fails.

Everybody, including the teen-ager loves a story, and students' choices of favorite poems prove this again and again. Joe begs his teacher to read aloud "The Highwayman," John selects "Casey at the Bat," and Susie memorizes all of Browning's "Pied Piper." The appeal of romance and adventure is universal. In anthologies like Stories in Verse[1] a wide variety of narrative poems appears.

Last in this brief list, but probably not least, is an interest in rhythm. Since the influence of the "hit tune" is strong, we may as well resign ourselves to Elvis Presley, his heirs and forebears, and capitalize on teen-agers' devotion to "crazy" rhythm. For the rock and roll fans, why not work up a "hot" choral reading version of Lindsay's "Daniel" or "The Congo"? For the amorous ballad addicts, Poe's "Annabel Lee"? For the military band or equestrian experts, Byron's "Destruction of Sennacherib" or Browning's "How They Brought the Good News from Ghent to Aix"?

On the basis of personal observation and experimentation, I would say that the best results in student reaction are achieved when poetry units or sections are introduced with selections carefully chosen to catch hold of one or more of these interest areas. Once the sympathies of the student are engaged, old antagonisms toward poetry begin to dissolve, and the teacher can lead on to new areas of interest because he has prepared the way. Some of these "old" antagonisms may stem from poor presentation of poetry in elementary school, natural perversity of intermediate boys (who dislike poetry because girls like it), or from a real inability to understand poetic language and structure.

Selection of poetry for reading and study involves other factors besides teen-age interests, however. It is not snobbish to look for poetic worth—some excellence or originality in style or treatment. It is snobbish to insist that such qualities are found only in so-called classic verse, the language and content of which may be obsolescent. We as teachers need to develop the catholicity of taste and breadth of reading background that will enable us to tolerate, and even enjoy, variety in poetry. When, in our selection of poetry, we are guided only by pet prejudices, we are wronging the student—we are passing on to him nothing but our own ignorance and narrow-mindedness. Every teacher has his preferences, his enthusiasms—some of them he may impart to his students, but some may not "go over" as he had hoped. This is the time to widen the horizon and cultivate within himself the capacity for new appreciations and new areas of interest. By example only, the teacher can assist the student to take part in the poetic interests of others and to share his own preferences in a mutually stimulating experience.

When we consider the differences in the reading levels of John, tenth grade, Susie, fourteenth plus, and Joe, fourth grade—all high school students—it becomes apparent that selection of poetry must be based also on individual differences in reading ability. Joe may have to start with "There Once Was a Puffin," "Jonathan Bing," and "Pirate Don Durk of Dowdee" from One Hundred Best Poems for Boys and Girls[2] or with a collection like the Benéts' Book of Americans[3] or with Edward Lear's limericks. By the time he has raised his reading level to sixth or seventh grade, he will enjoy "Three Peas on a Barrelhead" from Poems for a Machine Age,[4] though he will not understand every word of it. Likewise, he will be able to chant Benét's "Jesse James" with enthusiasm and Lindsay's "Simon Legree' with satanic gusto.

John will tell you emphatically that he "hates" poetry (some early traumatic educational experience, no doubt) and will glumly dare you to make him like it. Or he may sit apathetically waiting for this torture to pass, believing that "the less said the better." However, some of his antagonism will vanish when he finds out that he doesn't have to "get up and read the stuff" to the class. And when "teach" lets them choose any poem they'd like to have read, he puts in for "The Cremation of Sam McGee." Later he wants "Old Ironsides" or "Jonathan Moulton" or perhaps "The Wreck of the Hesperus." John is surprising and rather inconsistent in his choices, and usually he can't decide whether he likes a poem until he hears teacher read it aloud. Eventually he may even memorize "Eldorado" or "O Captain! My Captain!"

Susie follows the more "accepted" and traditional pattern of American literary taste—Shakespeare, Tennyson, Longfellow, Bryant, etc. But she needs a splash of Whitman, Dickinson, Millay, Benét, and Browning—to mention only a few. Often she studies poetry from the standpoint of duty rather than preference, and usually any dislike she may have for verse is not flaunted openly. Possessing the ability to paraphrase superficial meanings neatly, Susie needs to be led into thinking with greater insight and sharing as well as discerning emotions beneath the surface. Susie is probably more swayed by what teacher thinks because she understands more of what teacher

Non-Fiction for the Adolescent 93

is talking about. Here lies a threat to Susie's own freedom of thinking. Poetry "for tall people only" can help to blast Susie out of her rather self-satisfied rut. Susie needs to go far—much farther than John and Joe can ever manage—so for her we suggest much more poetry to read and much more mature subject matter and reading level. Yet she, too, needs to laugh and to learn the greatness of utter simplicity. (See list for Susie at end.)

Providing Variety

In some schools John, Susie, and Joe are in separate classes, but in most places heterogeneous grouping prevails. Regardless of this difference in arrangement, all students need to experience variety in poetry along several lines. Theme and subject variety is indispensable in the selection of poetry for teen-agers. They become bored by too much of anything. Nature poems they enjoy, but enough is enough—they'd also like to sample some love poems, a narrative or two, a ballad, a limerick, a sad lament on death, or a nonsense rhyme. In like manner they need to read poems that differ in style—meter, rhyme scheme, form, and type—a bit of everything from the ode to the hokku. Here is a marvelous opportunity to correlate the poetry selections with music of varied moods and types.

Because of narrow selection by some teachers and in some textbook-type anthologies, many students have the idea that all poetry was written in the dim past; variety in period of poems will help dispel this error and will give students a knowledge of the continuing creative urge which is still expressing itself in poetic form in our day. Variety in period will also illustrate to them the common hopes and dreams, fears and dreads faced by human beings since time began.

Students' individual tastes in poetry can be drawn upon to strike another note of variety. It is important for them to learn that not everyone has to like the same types of poems. Identical appreciation is not the goal; rather, a sharing and a broadening, not a standardization of taste.

Important, too, in developing a sense of unity with the past and present is the selection of poetry by writers of different nationalities. To give the student a sense of many literary traditions is to prepare him to live more realistically and appreciatively in his world. He should learn to understand that while English and American poets may be the most familiar to him, they are not the only poets who have written. Through the use of translations in textbooks and anthologies of world literature these poets of other lands (strange, many times, even to the teacher) may be added to the student's background. Here is an opportunity to draw upon the students' varying national origins to furnish links to the poetry of the world. To start on somewhat familiar ground in this study, try bits of Omar Khayyam, "Look to This Day" from the Sanskrit, and Goethe's "Erl King."

By attempting variety in selection, the teacher takes on the added opportunity and problem of extending students' knowledge of our common heritage. Allusions, whether obvious or subtle, mean little to a person whose general knowledge is distinguished only by its general poverty. I am reminded of thirty-five sophomores who pondered for some time over the phrase, "kill the fatted calf." Lack of interest in poetry, for John and Joe at least, may often originate with this matter of allusions. Wider reading in mythology, the Bible, fine arts, history, as well as all other fields is imperative in our ever-widening world. Part of the solution lies in using supplementary reading such as Herzberg's Myths and Their Meaning,[5] which relates the stories and characters of mythology (Greek, Roman, Norse, and Celtic) to literature and the arts, especially to passages of poetry. And many times the Mother Goose rhymes as well as our own American folk tales provide subject matter or figures of speech for the poets. Since these tales and jingles are not absorbed so much in the home and through the earlier grades as they were formerly, someone will have to lend a helping hand along the way to John, Susie, and Joe. That someone may well be the high school English teacher who is spreading before her class a varied diet of poetry.

To help motivate the student toward a wider reading background in both prose and poetry, the teacher will do well to capitalize on local talent or interests. Who wouldn't do better teaching the

Pike County ballads in Pike County? Why not teach Vachel Lindsay to natives of Springfield, Illinois? And statistics tell us that T. A. Daly goes over "big" with New York City high school students. The folklore and poetry of the students' own region always seem more interesting to them. Even the most ignorant or antagonistic student may be caught up by a familiar place name in a ballad. In this respect, books like Botkin's Treasury of American Folklore[6] supply facinating and exhaustive background reading.

Oral Reading

Another important consideration in selecting poetry is the range of possibilities for reading aloud. Teacher is expected to be able to read poetry effectively, but John, Joe, and Susie may be self-conscious on this score. Reading together as a class is one way to ease their tension, but blank verse, for example, does not usually lend itself to choral interpretation. Choose, rather poetry with pronounced repetition or rhythm, e. g., Lindsay's "Daniel"; also, ballads like "Barbara Allen," "Jesse James" (1910), or "Casey Jones," with their story and regular stanza form, read well aloud. Antiphonal poems such as "Lord Randal" provide a simple but interesting variation for choral practice. The Reading Chorus[7] or other similar books contain appropriate selections and add markings for suggested effects.

Especially with younger or less able students it is important to begin reading together poems which are somewhat familiar and which do not have an over-supply of "hard" words. By "hard" I mean polysyllabics, unusual names, coined words (like Poe's "tintinnabulation"), known words with unfamiliar meanings (e. g., "tells his tale" meaning "counts his number of sheep"), and words which describe concepts or experiences foreign to the student. Every poem has some of these, of course, but for beginning choral readers avoid picking poems in which such words abound. Success and enjoyment on a first attempt will tend to create more willingness on the part of the group to tackle harder and longer poems.

The Librarian's Role

Now a word to the librarian. To build a poetry shelf of maximum usefulness to the English department, consultation over book selection is of budgetary importance. There is no necessity for duplicating sets of books owned by the department. Also, anthologies of poetry should be selected which have the largest number of poems appealing to the particular school group for which they are intended. For "brains" like Susie I would suggest a collection like The Hollow Reed by Wrinn,[8] Poet's Handbook by Wood,[9] or Poems for Modern Youth by Gillis and Benet.[10] Earlier I mentioned other anthologies which have been used effectively for various class situations and levels of students. (See also lists at end.)

Individual authors such as Frost, Masefield, Millay, Eliot, Sandburg, Lindsay—to mention only a few—should certainly be represented in the library by collections and by biographies of the poets suited to high school reading—not a second-hand "Men of Letters" set.

The librarian can add interest to the teacher's poetry units by related displays of special poetry material—books, pictures, magazine or newspaper clippings, student-written poems, reports on poets, etc. Also, the library could maintain a collection of poetry records, professional and student, group and individual readings. Records of music correlated with poetry of various types should be added to this collection. A picture file of mounted prints of paintings and sculpture related to the study of poetry would prove most useful. For example, what senior wouldn't visualize Keats's Grecian urn more adequately if he could see a picture of one? Not all textbooks thoughtfully include such items.

It would seem that the English department should own at least one set of an anthology which combines analysis with selections, such as Untermeyer's Doorways to Poetry.[11] Most Untermeyer collections, in fact, are well-balanced in variety of selection and have analyses simple enough yet stimulating for high school students.

To finish on an essentially practical note, I have listed some books of poetry and verse which John, Susie, and Joe may enjoy and through which they may extend their appreciation of the world within and without.

For Susie:

Coffin, Robert P. Tristram. Selected Poems. Macmillan, 1955.

Non-Fiction for the Adolescent

Mac Leish, Archibald. Land of the Free. Harcourt, Brace, 1938.
Robinson, Edward Arlington. Collected Poems. Macmillan, 1927.
Masters, Edgar Lee. Songs and Satires. Macmillan, 1916.
DelaMare, Walter. Selected Poems. Henry Holt, 1927.
Shapiro, Karl. Essay on Rime. Reynal & Hitchcock, 1945.
Dunbar, Paul Lawrence. Complete Poems. Dodd, Mead, 1940.
Frost, Robert. Complete Poems. Henry Holt, 1949.
Wilkinson, Marguerite. New Voices: An Introduction to Contemporary Poetry. Macmillan, 1930.
Brown, Sharon, ed. Poetry of Our Times. Scott, Foresman, 1928.
Untermeyer, Louis. The Forms of Poetry: A Pocket Dictionary of Verse. Harcourt, Brace, 1936.
Spencer, Hazelton, ed. Selected Poems of Vachel Lindsay. Macmillan, 1931.
Hosford, Dorothy. By His Own Might: The Battles of Beowulf. Henry Holt, 1947.
Daringer, Helen F. and Easton, Anne T. The Poet's Craft. World Book Co., 1935.
Sandburg, Carl. Poems of the Midwest. World Publ. Co., 1946.
Teasdale, Sarah. Flame and Shadow. Macmillan, 1926.
Love Songs, Macmillan, 1926.
Helen of Troy and Other Poems. Macmillan, 1926.
Millay, Edna St. Vincent. Harp Weaver and Other Poems. Harper, 1923.
Second April. Harper, 1921.
A Few Figs From Thistles. Harper, 1922.
Renascence. Harper, 1917.
Conversation at Midnight. Harper & Bros., 1937.
Masefield, John. Poems. Macmillan, 1953.
Monroe, Harriet and Henderson, Alice Corbin. The New Poetry. Macmillan, 1923.

For John:

Brewton, John E. Under the Tent of Sky: A Collection of Poems About Animals Large and Small. Macmillan, 1937.
Sandburg, Carl. Poems of the Midwest. World Publ. Co., 1946.
Untermeyer, Louis, ed. The Pocket Book of Robert Frost's Poems. Pocket Books, Inc., 1946.
Untermeyer, Louis, ed. Stars to Steer By. Harcourt, Brace, 1941.
Thwing, Walter E. Best Loved Story Poems. Garden City Publ. Co., 1941.
Untermeyer, Louis, ed. The Magic Circle: Stories and People in Poetry. Harcourt, Brace, 1952.
Spencer, Hazelton, ed. Selected Poems of Vachel Lindsay. Macmillan, 1931.
Schauffler, Robert H., ed. The Poetry Cure: A Pocket Medicine Chest of Verse. Dodd, Mead, 1936.
Sarett, Lew. Collected Poems. Henry Holt, 1941.
Johnson, James Weldon, ed. Book of American Negro Poetry. Harcourt, Brace, 1931.
Service, Robert W. Ballads of a Chechako. New York: Barse & Hopkins, 1909.

Malone, Ted, comp. The American Album of Poetry. Morrow, 1938.
Neihardt, John G. Song of the Indian Wars. Macmillan, 1926.

For Joe:

Aldis, Dorothy. All Together: A Child's Treasury of Verse. G. P. Putnam's Sons, 1952.
McCord, David. Far and Few: Rhymes of the Never Was and Always Is. Little, Brown, 1952.
Barrows, Marjorie, comp. A Book of Famous Poems. Racine, Wis.: Whitman Publ. Co., 1931.
Service, Robert W. Rhymes of a Rolling Stone. Triangle Books, 1940.
Stuart, Jesse. Kentucky Is My Land. E. P. Dutton, 1952.
Brewton, John E. Under the Tent of Sky. Macmillan, 1937.
Sarett, Lew. Collected Poems. Henry Holt, 1941.

Notes

1. Hohn, Max T., ed. Stories in Verse (New York: Odyssey Press, 1943).

2. Barrrows, Marjorie, comp. One Hundred Best Poems for Boys and Girls (Racine, Wis.: Whitman Publ. Co., 1935).

3. Benét, Rosemary and Stephen Vincent. A Book of Americans (New York: Farrar and Rinehart, 1933).

4. McNeil, Horace J., ed. Poems for a Machine Age (New York: McGraw-Hill, 1941).

5. Herzberg, Max. Myths and Their Meaning (New York: Allyn and Bacon, 1931).

6. Botkin, B. A., ed. Treasury of American Folklore (New York: Crown, 1944).

7. Hicks, Helen G. The Reading Chorus (New York: Noble & Noble, 1939).

8. Wrinn, Mary J. J. The Hollow Reed (New York: Harper & Bros. 1935).

9. Wood, Clement. Poet's Handbook (New York: Garden City Publ. Co., 1942).

10. Gillis, Adolph and Benét, Wm. Rose. Poems for Modern Youth (New York: Houghton Mifflin, 1938).

11. Untermeyer, Louis. Doorways to Poetry (New York: Harcourt, Brace & Co., 1938).

"Astronomy Books for Children" by Donald and Elizabeth Macrae, Top of the News, 18:62-69, May, 1962. Reprinted with the permission of the American Library Association.

Undoubtedly, the excitement of Sputnik in 1957 and of the more recent space shots has been shared by the children, but it cannot explain all of their current interest in science. The sale of play space suits has fallen off, but the requests for science books continue.

It would seem that most children at a certain age are intuitive scientists and that we adults, in our new enthusiasm for acquainting the children with science—an enthusiasm born sometimes of fear, sometimes of business acumen, but sometimes of a clearer understanding of children's interests—have at last begun to tell our children what children have always wanted to know.

What they want to know in their early school years is everything about the world around them, everything from snakes to stars. They want the old fairy tales, books about prehistoric animals and early man, and books about veteran cars. Time is foreshortened for them. No wonder, then, that children like astronomy, which must look back in time to look out into the universe around.

Although astronomy is itself the oldest of sciences, it beckons the children excitingly into the future. It will be a future of space travel, of course, but, just as appealingly, it will be a future when perhaps the secret of the beginning of things will be unfolded in all its grandeur and orderliness.

Many authors use the historical method of presenting astronomy to children, and this is good. "I want a detective story, " said an eight-year-old, and he was given one. "No, " said he, "I want the important ones about the world and the stars!" The early Greek and Egyptian "detectives" in astronomy must be treated with respect, no matter how erroneous their conclusions. Gallant's Exploring the Universe is marred by his scorn for the Greek golden age scientists.

What is a child's first astronomical interest? The constellations used to be considered the primary step but, except possibly for the stories connected with them, this interest comes later. It seems likely that the child's first interest will mirror primitive man's first concern, the sun or lack of it, day and night, and, going on from there, the seasons. Or, taking the sun for granted, he might notice first the moon in the night sky.

Questions about the moon and sun undoubtedly pose themselves to the child long before he can read adequately, if at all. It would seem better to give his parent and him a book they could look at together rather than to offer one of the new picture-book controlled vocabulary variety.

The "Let's-read-and-find-out" series is titled optimistically insofar as those books on astronomy are concerned. The choice of subject is good but they are disappointingly written and illustrated. There is a point beyond which simplification leads to smugness if not to absurdity.

Consider The Moon Seems to Change by F. M. Branley, illustrated by Helen Borten. (F. M. Branley is the author of the very good book Mars written for young adults). This simple book seems to end in complete confusion, having attempted to explain the size, distance, and particularly the phases of the moon. The time required to reach the moon in a car is estimated and is off by a factor of ten, unless the car were to travel at the rate of a tricycle. The moon appears, in each of its phases, apparently to be seen from the same window. The child is urged to look for himself and see the moon in all of these phases. If he were to try, he would need to stay up until four in the morning to see one of the phases illustrated.

These overly simple books, What Makes Day and Night, The Moon Seems to Change, The Sun Our Nearest Star, are neither fish nor fowl. They do not lend themselves to being read aloud by a parent to a very young child. They are foolishly garrulous. They have no information or excitement to offer the alert six-year old who is beginning to read for himself. At best, then they are practice reading books, but dull.

Non-Fiction for the Adolescent

The book Space by Marian Tellander avoids the dilemma by attempting just enough more than the others to offer something not completely obvious. The illustrations are quieter, more informative, more conventional.

The Role of Illustrations

Illustrations are of prime importance in any science book, and especially in those for the younger readers. If the illustrations in The Moon Seems To Change could have been as beautiful and as carefully done as were Helmut Wimmer's for Branley's more mature The Moon, Earth's Natural Satellite, the limited text would have been more acceptable. Instead, in an apparent attempt to look childlike, they are sloppy and garish. No matter how bright and unlikely are the colors children use in their own work, there is usually an overall soft-spoken quality about it. The sun in The Moon Seems to Change looks like an angry daisy reaching out to envelop the avocado-green moon. The whole thing somehow fails to convey the serene beauty of our moon as she 'walks the night.' There is little sense of wonder.

In the books intended particularly for young children, the illustrations should convey something of the majesty and vastness of space. Colored charts and diagrams add life and clarity to the text, but there seems little advantage in the almost universal portrayal of Jupiter as a gay beach ball.

One of the accepted conventions is to show the moon upside down, as it appears in the telescope, but it should not be reversed also as on page 16 of Grey's First Book of Astronomy. A picture of a solar eclipse with the shadow sharply defined is often used erroneously to illustrate a lunar eclipse. The latter can be demonstrated best in color, to show the reddening.

As in all books, the illustrations and text should be consistent. On page 50 of Branley's Nine Planets the text, which does not distinguish between oppositions and favorable oppositions, limits the close approaches of Mars to many fewer than the very clear diagram by Helmut Wimmer shows.

One look at a good picture of the earth in space will bring the question, "What holds it up?" Some books have been satisfied with throwing in the magic word "gravity" in italics or capital letters and perhaps buttressed with an exclamation point, but this, without further explanation, only thickens the plot. So inevitable is the question and so fundamental the answer that the treatment of the subject might serve as a kind of touchstone by which to judge the books. A great number of books, although setting out to be introductory, simply ignore the problem and launch into a detailed description of planetary orbits. Freeman's Fun with Astronomy sidesteps the question. "Nowadays we know the earth is not held up by anything... and moves through space in a special way."

You among the Stars by Herman and Nina Schneider was one of the first books to undertake to explain the fundamental forces. It takes care to describe gravity and then says, "It is the sun's gravity that keeps the earth in its path around the sun. It pulls just strongly enough to keep the earth exactly in place." There is no mention of why it is pulling.

The Golden Book of Astronomy by Wyler and Ames devotes more time to the question and answers it clearly and succinctly, but uses the concept that "centrifugal force" balances the pull of gravity.

All about the Planets by Patricia Lauber uses a more mature but precise vocabulary and her answer is pleasingly clear. "A planet's movement results from the balance of two forces. One is inertia—the tendency to keep moving forever in a straight line. The other is gravity—the pull of the sun. Without the sun's gravity the planet would fly off into space. Without inertia, it would be drawn into the fiery mass of the sun. The balance of the two forces keeps the planet moving around the sun in its orbit." It is worth while to compare the foregoing with The Nine Planets by F. M. Branley in which, on page 16, there is a confusing attempt to use non-scientific terms in order to be understood.

It seems imperative that some precise scientific terms be introduced, explained, and used consistently. For a further discussion of this, we refer you to the article "Space Books—Which Ones and Why," by Lloyd Motz and Minnie R. Motz, Top of the News, May, 1961; to the survey of children's science books in Natural History,

Non-Fiction for the Adolescent

December, 1961; to the Foreword of the AAAS <u>Science Book List for Children,</u> page viii; to <u>The Unreluctant Years</u> by Lillian Smith, page 182.

The authors of good astronomy books, as are the authors of any good books, are fired with enthusiasm, knowledge, and respect both for their subject and their readers. Too often the books seem to have been "done" rather than written with any pleasure and sense of cummunication. If the author has a clear picture of the specific level of interest he wants to inform, the material he chooses for inclusion will have a balance and evenness of treatment. Libration in latitude should not be undertaken for instance, in a book where the word "crater" must be defined.

Once the child has had some of his first questions answered satisfactorily for the time, and has caught a glimpse of the inexorable and fundamental laws of the universe, his interest turns to dimensions. How big? How far? Some authors take advantage of this with a kind of sensationalism, saying "billions and billions of miles" when "millions" is more nearly correct, or dealing in volumes rather than areas and diameters. The vastness of the universe does not need to be magnified.

Mistakes in Books

There are certain discrepancies among books which set forth, for instance, the distances from planets to sun or the diameters of the planets. These are superficial and unimportant, but they are often "corrected" in the library books by the children themselves. The diameter of Jupiter is given as 88,000 miles in <u>Fun with Astronomy,</u> as 88,700 in <u>Boys Book of Astronomy</u> by P. Moore, as 88,690 in <u>First Book of Astronomy.</u> All of these are equatorial measurements and are acceptable approximate figures. However, the more appropriate 86,900 is the mean of the polar and equatorial figures and is the one given by Branley in <u>The Nine Planets.</u> He explains mean distances, and so does A. T. White in <u>All about the Stars,</u> and it is helpful when authors do.

Librarians will always have to do some verbal editing, however, as they use the books. It may be that, as a group, librarians tend to blanch at the word 'science'; but there is a need to catch up with our young readers. When such topics as relativity and antimatter are introduced into our older children's books without apology, there is some indication that we can understand more than we have always thought we could.

"This Universe of Space" by Peter M. Millman, eight radio lectures heard on CBC University of the Air, has peen (sic) published (1961) by the Canadian Broadcasting Corporation, Toronto, and is a clear presentation of pertinent information. Splendor in the Sky by G. S. Hawkins is good. The perennial authority Introduction to Astronomy by Robert H. Baker is now in its sixth edition.

The problem of book selection for science would be lessened by a wider knowledge on the part of librarians of some of the fundamentals of the subject, but they will have to rely on expert advice. The AAAS Science Book List for Children recommended in Top of the News, March, 1961, by Jane Davies, is disappointing. Indeed some of the books starred for first purchase in that list were those which were so wisely but adversely criticized by Miss Davies. There are many inclusions in the AAAS list of astronomy books which we cannot recommend.

The new edition of Stars for Sam by Maxwell Reed, edited by Paul F. Brandwein, is an example. The older edition, now out of date, was well written and well organized. The new one is disorganized. There has been some unfortunate rewriting of some sections. Compare the end of the paragraph on cepheid variables, old edition page 102, new edition page 124. On page 119, new edition, a light year is defined, and in the next paragraph the term is used incorrectly. On page 24 there is a full page lunar eclipse sequence which is described as "phases of the moon."

Recommended Books

The following is a list of books we found worthy of recommendation, sometimes with reservations. There are very few for the youngest readers insofar as text is concerned. However, there is a great deal to be said for the young children's enjoyment of good illustrations accompanying a more mature text. A librarian re-

Non-Fiction for the Adolescent 105

cently questioned the wisdom of a young borrower's choice of a science book. "Do you think you can really read that?" she asked. He looked at her and with withering scorn replied, "I can't <u>read</u> it. But I can understand it."

This list contains books printed some years ago as well as the newer ones. The basic knowledge and concepts of astronomy change slowly, and a book published five years ago can contain the whole body of well-established information. Old theories are relatively secure, but should never be presented as definitive. New theories are exciting, but they need to be presented tentatively, because they lack the necessary degree of confirmation. Indeed, the newer a theory the more likely it is to be modified, if not discarded; for example, the two Van Allen belts are now thought to be but one. Finally, a newly published book does not necessarily mean one with the latest theories. In fact, there are some which propagate long dead ideas, such as the one that the moon's place of origin was the Pacific Ocean.

Asimov, Isaac. <u>The Kingdom of the Sun.</u> Abelard, 1960.
> Historical approach to astronomy for readers who have a more mature interest; good selection of subject matter within the limits of 150 pages. Very few of the usual oversimplifications. Interesting style. Diagrams but no photographs. Poor paper.

Baker, Robert H. <u>When The Stars Come Out</u>, rev. ed., Viking, 1957.
> History of the science of astronomy. Constellations. Good illustrations.

Baker, Robert H. <u>Introducing the Constellations.</u> Viking, 1957.

Binder, Otto. <u>The Moon, Our Neighboring World.</u> Golden Press, 1961.
> Poor binding. Illustration on page 14 underlines the Pacific Ocean theory of the origin of the moon. However, it has a great deal of reliable information and some outstandingly good diagrams and photographs.

Binder, Ott. (sic) <u>Planet, Other Worlds of Our Solar System.</u> Golden Press, 1961.
> Poor binding for a library. With some few exceptions (E. G., comets are erroneously linked with asteroids) there is good

presentation of information. With each planet, there is a list of vital statistics, often wanted by children. The illustrations are used to convey auxillary information as well as to illustrate the text. Some information on the sun is included. Not as thorough a discussion of planetary formation theories as in Gallant's Exploring The Planets.

Branley, F. M. A Book of Planets for You, illus. by Leonard Kessler.
A factual book in which the information is accurate. Not an exciting presentation. Illustrations brilliantly colored and sloppy. The text states, "The rings of Saturn are very beautiful." The illustration scarcely bears this out. For young readers.

Branley, F. M. The Moon, Earth's Natural Satellite, illus. by Helmut Wimmer. Crowell, 1960.
Beautiful and, for the most part, accurate illustrations. Text disorganized and repetitious. Mixture of elementary and advanced information.

Fenton, C. L. Worlds in the Sky. Day, 1950.
The facts of astronomy rather than the theories. Attractive format and style.

Freeman, Mae and Ira. Fun with Astronomy. Random, 1953.
The only book at this level with simple experiments to illustrate principles.

Gallant, Roy A. Exploring Mars. Doubleday, 1956.
Planetary formations in general and the known facts about Mars. Exciting illustrations. (The format of all of Gallant's books is attractive to all ages of children, even into Junior High School. The treatment of the subjects is mature enough to interest the older children. Some of his illustrators are more successful than others.)

Gallant, Roy A. Exploring the Moon. Doubleday, 1956.
Emphasis on a now discarded view of the origin of the moon. The excellent photographs of the moon now available make these illustrations ordinary.

Gallant, Roy A. Exploring the Planets. Doubleday, 1958.
Theories on the formation of planets in more detail than in Exploring Mars. A great deal of information well presented

and illustrated. A more mature book than the others in the series.

Gallant, Roy A. Exploring the Sun. Doubleday, 1957.
More mature information than in Zim's book on the subject.

Gallant, Roy A. Exploring the Universe. Doubleday, 1956.
History of the theories of the origin of the universe presented with an unfortunate attitude toward the ancient astronomers. Otherwise good.

Gamow, George. The Moon. Abelard, 1959.
Professional physical scientist and a skillful writer with an interesting style. For older children.

Grey, V. The First Book of Astronomy. Watts, 1959.
A book similar in its aims to Worlds in the Sky, better illustrated but not as well written. Refraction is said to be the reason for the sky's blue color; actually, the air molecules scatter the sun's rays, the blue more than the red, so that in the daytime the atmosphere is suffused with bluish-tinted light. Explanation of earth's orbit similar to that of Golden Book of Astronomy.

Kees, Boeke. Cosmic View. Day, 1960.
Subtitle, The Universe in Forty Jumps. The first jumps are outward into space. A new and effective approach to the size of the universe.

La Paz, Lincoln and Jean. Space Nomads. Holiday House, 1961.
An astronomer and his daughter writing with excitement and pleasure about their work, mainly the study of meteorites. For older children. In this branch of astronomy, nomenclature is somewhat unsettled. Usually (but not in this book) a meteorite is a meteoroid which falls to the ground, while a meteor is one which is consumed in the earth's atmosphere and appears as a "shooting star." It is widely believed that the former are physically related to the asteroids, while the latter are the debris of comets.

Lauber, Patricia. All about the Planets. Random House, 1960.
The best book on the subject for this age group. Interesting style, no slurring over subtleties, competent discussions of all

the theories of the formation of the solar system. An up-to-date discussion of the surface of the moon.

Lauber, Patricia. The Quest of Galileo. Garden City, 1959.
A book associated with the subject of astronomy, clear discussion of Galileo's experiments on falling bodies.

May, Julian. Show Me the World of Astronomy. Pennington Press, 1959.
Very good pictures of the night sky in the part on constellations. The remainder of the book is full of errors.

Neely, Henry M. The Stars by Clock and Fist. Viking, 1956.
How to find and observe the stars.

Neurath, Marie. Wonders of the Universe. Max Parrish, 1961.
In the same format as the other Max Parrish color books. Easy-looking format, complex subjects, but well explained and illustrated. Types of stars and their life cycles. Sunspots and their magnetic fields. The red shift. Incomplete account of the formation of the earth and other planets.

Page, Lou Williams. A Dipper Full of Stars. rev. ed. Follett, 1959.
Subtitle, A Beginner's Guide to the Heavens. A book for an older amateur observer, with a good deal of authoritative information about what he will be looking at. Good treatment of the formation of the solar system. Good style.

Rey, H. A. Find the Constellations. Houghton, 1954.
Enjoyable, if slangy, style. Attractive format. Reproduction of actual night sky not as clear as in May's Show Me the World of Astronomy. Planet finder now out of date.

Rudaux, Lucien, and De Vaucouleurs, G. Larousse Encyclopedia of Astronomy, with an introduction by F. L. Whipple, Prometheus Press, 1959.
A one-volume encyclopedia with detailed authoritative information and fine illustrations, some in color.

Schneider, Herman and Nina. You among the Stars. Scott, 1951.
Poor illustrations of astronomical objects, but persuasive pictures of children looking at a night sky.

Schneider, Leo. Space in Your Future. Harcourt, 1961.
The solar system and the tools of an astronomer in great de-

tail. Very good for older children. Experiments.

Shepherd, Walter. The Universe. Longacre, 1960.
Double columns, clear print, good illustrations. Theory of relativity introduced with some success.

Tellander, Marian. Space. Follett, 1960.
Twenty-four pages of restricted vocabulary which undertakes a simple introduction to the solar system, Milky Way, and some constellations. The sun in all illustrations is too small.

White, A. T. All about the Stars. Random House, 1954.
"All about" the solar system and the stars. Very well written. "Traffic laws of the sky" a good explanation.

Wyler, Rose and Ames, Gerald. The Golden Book of Astronomy, rev. ed. Golden Press, 1959.
Excellent one-book introduction to all phases of astronomy from time and tides to space travel. Clear style. Good diagrams.

Zim, Herbert S. Comets. Morrow, 1957.

Zim, Herbert S. Shooting Stars. Morrow, 1958. Not one of his best.

Zim, Herbert S. The Sun. Morrow. 1953. The sun's effect upon the earth.

Zim, Herbert S. The Universe. Morrow, 1961.
Sixty-four pages to deal with the history, methods of investigation, theories of the universe, types of stars. He manages to introduce all of these in a way that will arouse interest.

Zim, Herbert S. and Baker, Robert H. Stars. Simon and Schuster, 1961.
Subtitle, A Guide to the Constellations, Sun, Moon, Planets, and Other Features of the Heavens. Profusion of colored charts and illustrations.

"Books About Negroes for Children" by Charlamae Rollins, ALA Bulletin, 53:306-308, April, 1959. Reprinted with the permission of the American Library Association.

The first edition of the pamphlet We Build Together, published in 1941 by the National Council of Teachers of English, listed only 72 titles of acceptable books about Negroes for children of elementary school age. In 1948 a second edition included 90 children's books dealing with Negro life.

In 1949 Mrs. Augusta Baker, assistant coordinator of work with children and supervisor of storytelling in the New York Public Library, published a pamphlet, Books about Negro Life for Children, which included 95 books about American Negroes for children. Her latest pamphlet, published in 1957 with the assistance of a Dutton-Macrae Award, critically evaluates more than two hundred excellent books about American Negroes for children.

The purpose of this article is to point up the progress that has been made in the field of writing, illustrating, and publishing books about Negroes for children in the last ten years. In addition, it is hoped that librarians, teachers, parents, and others interested in selecting books to meet a specific need will also find some help here.

For those who are unaware of the sensitive areas in writing about Negroes for children, a brief summary of the criteria used in the pamphlets cited above may be helpful.

1. Books with illustrations that stereotype or ridicule the Negro child are objectionable. These are known as "pickaninny pictures."

2. Books that use terms of derision such as "nigger," "darkey," "coon," "spook," "Rastus," "Sambo," and "pickaninny."

There are exceptions to this. In historical fiction for older children where the characters are known to have used these terms, this is accepted. An author who tries to present an honest portrayal of a period must of necessity set down the words as they were naturally used. In order to recreate certain scenes in a particular setting he must try to give a faithful presentation. Examples of this may be found in Railroad to Freedom, by Hildegard Swift (Harcourt, Brace) and the more recent Newbery Award winner Rifles for Watie by Harold Keith (Crowell).

The real objection to these terms arises when the author uses them in referring to his characters. Examples of this unconscious stereotyping are: "The ancient darkey scratched his kinky head." "The fat black cook waddled into the kitchen." "An engaging pickaninny rolled on the dirty cabin floor." "The terrified coons scuttled for cover." The home of a poor Negro is a "cabin." The Negro minor character never smiles or laughs, he "grins widely." All Negroes have "pearly white teeth."

3. The use of heavy dialect in children's books has been discussed widely. No honest author of children's books uses it simply as a handy gimmick to delineate a character, whether he is a villain, a Negro, or any minor character.

Recently a supervisor of children's work in a large midwestern city wrote to the publisher of the Doctor Dolittle books when a member of her staff questioned the value of replacing them because of the objectionable language. The reply happily brought out the fact that the latest edition of the Doctor Dolittle books no longer includes the words she referred to. The publisher deplored their use as much as others did, but revision, especially of books by an author who is no longer living, presents difficult problems.

Publishers are reconsidering their older books in the light of such inquiries, and alert librarians in re-evaluation for replacement have a fine opportunity to make certain that in considering older books for repurchase the book collection keeps pace with the present-day interpretation of human relations.

We Build Together made a plea for heroes for Negro children—books about real people. This need is now being adequately met by a yearly output of at least a half-dozen individual biographies of eminent Negroes, past and present. There are also useful special collections of biographies, such as Famous Negro Music Makers by Hughes (Dodd, Mead) and general biography collections notable for their inclusion of all the important persons in a particular field regardless of race. An example is Giants of Jazz by Terkel (Crowell). Elizabeth Yates was awarded the Newbery Medal in 1951 for Amos Fortune: Free Man (Aladdin), a splendid hero story for any child above the fourth grade.

Several good books have been written, both nonfiction and fiction, about Harriet Tubman, the slave woman who led more than two hundred of her people to freedom. Mary McCleod Bethune and Marian Anderson are also popular subjects.

A really notable book of 1958 was Captain of the Planter by Sterling (Doubleday). This is a thrilling and fully documented account of the unlettered slave boy who boldly sailed the Planter, a Confederate ship, into the hands of the Union Army.

In poetry and in fiction Negro children are encouraged when they see reflections of themselves. Gwendolyn Books' Bronzeville Boys and Girls (Harper) and the merry folk rhymes and games of Margaret Taylor's Did You Feed My Cow? (Crowell) are especially cherished by Negro children, although they are enjoyed by all boys and girls.

For older girls, Florence Means, well known for her earlier pioneering in this field, has written Reach for a Star (Houghton Mifflin), significant because it is the only story which gives a picture of life at a large coeducational Negro university. It is a warm and wholesome love story as well. Miriam Blanton has written a girl's story, Hold Fast to Your Dreams (Messner), about the trials faced by a Negro girl who longed to be a ballet dancer. This story also touches the problem of school integration in the Midwest. Julie's Heritage by Catherine Marshall (Longmans) is a story of the problems that beset a Negro girl in a northern city. Hope Newell has written two popular stories about Mary Ellis, a Negro student nurse who trained in a white hospital, A Cap for Mary Ellis and Mary Ellis Student Nurse (Harper). The Barred Road (Macmillan) by DeLeeuw is a story of the friendship between a white and Negro girl that withstood the pressures of a hostile community.

Writers of books on sports, both fiction and nonfiction, have kept pace with the gains that have been made by Negroes in the major sports fields—baseball, football, basketball, boxing, and track. Among the many successful writers of sports books are John Tunis, Gregor Felsen, Duane Decker, Jesse Jackson and C. H. Frick. Gilbert Douglas in Hard to Tackle, a football story, successfully combines the sports element with a community problem.

A bold venture in the field of stories for junior high-school boys and girls is New Dreams for Old by Person (Longmans), a present-day story of youth in the Deep South which provides an easily understood view of the economic as well as the cultural changes there. Equally courageous is South Town by Graham (Follett), a story of the hardships faced by an ambitious Negro boy in a small southern community. The important message of this moving story is one of hope for the future when there will be greater understanding between the two races in the South.

The progress of the past ten years reported here is a real tribute to the conscious effort that has been made by hundreds of workers with children and children's books.

Scores of selective lists have been prepared. Among the many now available are:

Books about Negro Life for Children, Augusta Baker. New York Library, 1957.

Books Are Bridges, The American Friends Service Committee and the Anti-Defamation League of B'nai B'rith, 1957.

Brotherhood Lists, The National Conference of Christians and Jews.

Reading Ladders for Human Understanding, by Margaret Heaton, Washington, American Council on Education, 1955.

Part Four. Problems in Adolescent Literature

Four areas which present problems in literature for adolescents have been chosen for discussion: censorship, junior novels, series in fiction, and comic books. Three are problems of selection while the fourth, comics, is really a matter of guidance.

Censorship. There is considerable evidence to show that there has been a decided increase in censorship activities in recent years. The National Education Association has pointed out that the public schools have been the target of much criticism and censorship, with the John Birch Society the number one troublemaker. The NEA reported that, as a result of criticism from these groups, 29% of the questionable books were removed, 50% were retained, and 21% of the books were held for further study. In a 1963 survey of Wisconsin public schools, Dr. Lee A. Burress reported that there was a censorship incidence of about 20%; that is, about one-fifth of the schools responding to this survey said they had encountered problems of this nature. It is very clear, then, that the possibility of censorship is far too great for the librarian to ignore the problem.

Junior Novels. The junior, or adolescent, novel had its origin in the series books that enjoyed tremendous popularity during the latter part of the nineteenth century and the early part of this century. Written especially for young people, these junior novels make up a good proportion of the fiction collection of the typical high school library. Just as in the earlier series books, there are often serious questions about the quality of the books being produced. Trite plots, shallow characterizations, and weak themes are common complaints of librarians, classroom teachers, and sometimes students.

Series. Chosen for discussion here has been the fiction series, rather than non-fiction. Perhaps it is not even a serious selection problem in most libraries—but rather a problem of justifying to the youthful patron the library's policy of not purchasing Nancy Drew,

Hardy Boys, or the Bobbsey Twins. For historical information on the series, it is suggested that the article "For It Was Indeed He" in Fortune, April, 1934, be read.

Comic Books. Whether or not we accept the condemnation of comic books by Frederic Wertham in Seduction Of The Innocent, most librarians agree that it is desirable to guide the youngster into better reading than is offered by the comics. Dwight Burton offers assistance in choosing transitional material in the final article of part four.

"Censorship and the Values of Fiction" by W. C. Booth. English Journal, 53:155-164, March, 1964. Reprinted with the permission of the National Council of Teachers of English.

To the teacher, any attempt by outsiders to censor teaching materials is self-evidently wrong. To the censor, it is self-evident that a responsible society must supervise what is taught to its children. Little wonder, then, that attacks on "censorship," like defenses of "responsible supervision of materials," too often assume what they set out to prove: addressed to those who are already converted, they may be useful for enspiriting the troops, but far too often they do nothing to breach the enemy's line.

To convert any "enemy," we must show him not simply that respectability, or tradition, or the National Council of Teachers of English are against him but that he is wrong, wrong according to his own fundamental standards. To tell him that he is wrong according to our standards gets us nowhere, though it may be great fun; the problem is to find, somewhere among his standards, at least one that is violated by what he proposes to do.

In dealing with censors, as with other enemies, it may very well be that the enemy is in fact so far beyond reason that there is no possible point of contact. But if we assume, as I think we must, that at least some of the would-be censors are men of goodwill whose values, at certain points, coincide with ours, then we must work at the extremely difficult task of showing them that even according to their own values, the effort to censor is misguided.

The sources for such points of contact—and hence of real rather than merely self-comforting arguments—are many. Most censors want to preserve some form of society in which they can exercise their own freedom; we can argue, following Mill and many others, that the kind of society the censor really wants cannot be maintained if his kind of censorship prevails. Similarly, most censors respect and seek to further the "truth" as they see it, and some of them can be shaken by arguing, with Milton and others, that truth flourishes best when ideas can compete freely. Or again, many censors, irrational as they may seem to us, respect consistency and would like to think of themselves as reasonable; they can be shaken, sometimes, by showing the inevitable irrationalities and stupidities committed by any society that attempts to censor.

Every teacher in America today owes it to himself to have ready, either in his mind or in his files, a portfolio of these and other arguments against censorship, fleshed out, of course, with the details that alone can make them convincing. He can never know when the censors will move in his direction, nor can he know in advance which of his supply of arguments will be effective in a given crisis. But he can know that unless he has thought the issues through, he is likely, when the attack comes, to stand tongue-tied. Of course he may go under anyway, no matter how well-prepared his defense, if the censor will not listen to his reasons; one should have no illusions about the easy triumph of freedom or truth, in any market place, open or closed. But even if the censor wins, there should be some comfort in knowing that one has at least said what can be said for the free teacher, freely choosing his own materials.

Specific Defenses Necessary

Since many censorship drives begin with attacks on specific works, an important and often neglected section of one's "Freedom Portfolio" ought to deal with some such heading as "The Moral Quality of Individual Works." Though censorship cases are seldom fought without some appeal to general political and social arguments that apply to all cases, they would more often be won if, at the first threat of attack on any one work, the teacher had a battery of specific defenses ready for battle.

What is usually offered, in place of such specific arguments, is a standard collection of highly general claims, already known to the censor, about the moral value of literature. There is good reason why such claims do not convince. For one thing, some literature is not moral, and there is even much good—that is, clever—literature which is quite obviously at odds with any moral values the censor can

Problems in Adolescent Literature

be expected to care about. For another, most literature, even of the most obviously moral kind, is potentially harmful to somebody, as Thomas Hardy pointed out in defense of Tess of the D'Urbervilles. The censors are thus always on safe ground, from their own point of view, so long as we talk about all literature, or even all "good" literature. Even the most ridiculous attacks—say those on Robin Hood—have this much validity: it is conceivable that such a work might alter a child's beliefs, and if we admit this, we must also admit that the alteration might be "for the worse," according to the censor's values. The child who reads Robin Hood might decide to rob from the rich and give to the poor, or he might even decide to support a progressive income tax. We do no service to our cause if we pretend, as some have done, that literature cannot have such effects because it does not deal with beliefs. Any literary work that we really read will play upon our basic beliefs, and even though fundamental changes of belief produced by novels may be rarer among mature readers than among novices, it would be foolish to pretend that they do not occur. If the change is "for the worse," from the censor's point of view, then the work has done harm, and it should be banned.

In contrast to our general claims, the censor usually has some specific danger in mind which is directly and literally related to something he has seen in the text. He has found profanity or obscenity or depravity, and we tell him that the book will, like all "good books," do the students good. In Austin, Texas, a pastor who was testifying in a hearing against Andersonville read aloud a long sequence of cuss words, excerpted from widely separated bits of the novel. The committee was quite properly horrified. The book they "read" was a bad book by any criterion, and certainly it would be a bad book to teach. But the horrifying fact about the episode[1] is not that the committee members were offended by what they had heard but that none of them had enough gumption to read so much as a single page of the real book straight through. It would do no good to say to such committeemen, when the preacher was finished, that Andersonville is really a highly moral work; the "book" which they experienced was not. Similarly it does no good to say to the censor of The Catcher in the Rye that it is really "calling for a good world in which people can connect—a key word in twentieth-century writing."[2] One can picture the reactions of the irate parent who has discovered the obscenities in Catcher as he reads the following defense of the morality of fiction-in-general:

> When the student learns to see great books, classic or contemporary, as metaphors for the whole of human experience, the study of literature contributes in a unique way to this understanding of these traditions. They help him to discover who he is and where he is going.
>
> An abstraction may have little emotional impact. But the dramatization of an abstraction, of concepts and values, offers us something we can grasp. We begin to feel and understand the abstraction.[3]

Now here is something for the parent really to worry about: if Catcher is on his mind, he will think that we teachers are treating its profanity and obscenity as standing for "the whole of human experience," suitable to help his child "to understand who he is and where he is going"! It is surely no comfort to tell him that literature, by dramatizing the experience of profanity and obscenity, makes it have more emotional impact.

The obscene phrase that Holden tries to erase from the school walls toward the end of Catcher is concrete, literal, visible; our "defenses of poesie" tend to be abstract, metaphoric, intangible. We must somehow make them seem to the censor as real as the abuses he has found, but to do so will never be easy. To be concrete and specific about the moral values even of a short poem is terribly difficult, and the precise inferences through which a good reader constructs his reading of a complete novel are so complex that it is no wonder we draw back from the effort to describe them. Yet it is only by learning to follow such processes for himself—that is, by learning how to read—that the censor can discover what we really mean by the morality or immorality of a work. Unless those who wield educational power know at first hand what we mean when we say that a literary work can be moral even though many of its elements are to them objectionable, the other defenses against censorship may finally fail.

I have a frequently recurring fantasy in which I am called before a censorship committee and asked to justify my teaching of such-and-such a book. As hero of my own dream, I see myself starting on page one of whatever book is attacked and reading aloud, with commentary and discussion, page by page, day by day, until the censors either lynch me or confess to a conversion.

A pipedream, clearly. And the one I use for substitute is not much less fantastic. An irate committeeman comes to me (I am a very young instructor in a highly vulnerable school district), and he threatens to have me fired for teaching The Catcher in the Rye (or Huckleberry Finn, or Catch-22—one can of course mold one's daydreams to suit current events). I look him boldly in the eye and I ask him one question: "Will you, before you fire me, do me one last favor? Will you read carefully a little statement I have made about the teaching of this book, and then reread the book?" And since it is fantasy, he says, "Well, I don't see why not. I want to be reasonable." And away he goes, bearing my neatly-typed manuscript and my marked copy of Catcher. Some hours later he comes back, offers his humble apologies for what he calls his "foolish mistake," and returns my manuscript. Here it is.

What to Do With a Literary Work Before Deciding to Censor It

Let us begin by assuming that we ought to censor all books that we think are immoral. Learned men have offered many arguments against this assumption (you might want to take a look at Milton's Areopagitica, John Stuart Mill's On Liberty, or the NCTE pamphlet, The Students' Right to Read, a copy of which I can lend you), but other learned and wise men, like Plato and Tolstoy, have accepted it, and we can do the same—at least for a time. What should determine whether a book is among those we want to censor?

The question will not arise, of course, unless you have found, as in Catcher, something objectionable. There you have found such things as teenagers speaking profanities, the phrase "Fuck you"—repeated!—and a schoolboy visit to a prostitute. It must seem to you that I am being merely perverse when I say that such a book is really highly moral, when "read properly." Yet I mean something quite real and concrete by this claim. Unfortunately, to see fully what I mean you would need to sit in my classroom every day, throughout the time we spend trying to learn how to read Catcher "properly." I know that you cannot spend the time that would be required for this experience, and the principal probably wouldn't allow it even if you could. But there are certain things you can do, on your own, to discover what a "proper reading" of this book might be.

The big job is to relate the seemingly offensive passages to the context provided by the whole work. To say this is not, as you might think, merely a trick to sidestep the true issues. We all relate literary parts to their contexts all the time, almost without thinking about it. If someone told us that a book talked openly about nakedness, we might, if we are worried by pornography, begin to worry. But we are not troubled to read "I was a stranger, and ye took me in: Naked, and ye clothed me: I was sick, and ye visited me." The context has transformed both the word "naked" and the concept of nakedness to obviously moral uses. Similarly, when we read about the woman "taken in adultery," caught "in the very act," we do not ask that the reading be changed to something less specific. Not only do we take for granted the piety of the Bible—something we do not and cannot do for Catcher—but the immediate context in John viii quite evidently requires a forceful statement of the nature of the sin that is being forgiven. If you doubt this, try substituting some lesser sin—say gossiping—for adultery in the passage, or some euphemism like "caught flirting with another woman's husband."

When we read the many other specific accounts of sexual abuses that the Bible contains—of seduction, incest, sodomy, rape, and what not—we do not put the Bible on the list of banned books, because we know that the context requires an honest treatment of man's vices, and that it at the same time changes the very effect of naming them. Though we might question the wisdom of teaching particular sections of the Bible to children of a particular age, we would never think of firing a teacher simply for "teaching the Bible." We would want at the very least to know what the teacher was doing with it. We know the context, in this case, and consequently we know

Problems in Adolescent Literature 123

there is at least one book with many bad things in it that is still a good book.

It is exactly this same claim that we teachers want to make about a book like <u>Catcher in the Rye</u> (though few of us would want to go as far as one theologian who has called it a piece of "modern scripture"). But since the claim is much harder to substantiate with a long work like a novel, I want to begin with a look at how the process of transformation works in a short simple poem. Any poem with possibly offensive elements would do, but I have chosen a highly secular one that is likely to offend in several ways: "ugUDuh," by E. E. Cummings.

      ygUDuh

        ydoan
        yunnuhstan
        ydoan o
        yunnuhstan
        yguduh ged

        yunnuhstan dem doidee
        yguduh ged riduh
        ydoan o nudn

      LISN bud LISN

        dem
        gud
        am
        lil yelluh bas
        tuds weer goin
        duh SIVILEYEzum

This poem may very well seem unintelligible to you on first reading. I've seen a class of high school seniors flounder with it—until I asked one of them to read it aloud. But then they worked out something like the following "translation" (though there was usually some unresolved debate about whether it is spoken by one speaker or two):

      You've got to

      You don't
      Do you understand?
      You don't know
      Do you understand those
      You've got to get
      Do you understand? Those dirty
      You've got to get rid of

>   You don't know anything
>   LISTEN, Bud, LISTEN
>   Those
>   God
>   damn
>   little yellow bas-
>   tards, we're going
>   To CIVILIZE them.

Now that the poem is out in the open, as it were (though limping badly), it obviously offers several possible kinds of offense. We can imagine, first of all, a National Association for the Advancement of Yellow Peoples rising in protest against the offending phrase yellow bastards, just as the NAACP of Brooklyn had Huckleberry Finn banned because it refers to Jim constantly as Nigger Jim. What right has a poet to use such language, degrading a whole people? Even though the poem was obviously written in wartime, when tempers ran high, that is no excuse for descending to such abuse.

"The context of the whole poem" provides an answer to this imaginary protest. Does Cummings, the poet, call the Japanese "yellow bastards"? Obviously not. There is a speaker, dramatized for our literary observation, a speaker whose tongue bewrayeth him, with every half-word that speweth out of his mouth. It is this speaker from whom the whole content of our paraphrase comes: he it is who would take those yellow bastards and civilize them. What Cummings says, of course, is provided only by inference from the way in which the statement is conveyed. The speaker provides, in the many signs of his brutish inarticulateness, evidence that Cummings is as greatly opposed to his foolish bigotry as the president of the NAAYP might be. And of course, the poet expects us to take pleasure in the comic contrast between the speaker's lack of civilization and his bold program.

If the members of the NAAYP still feel dissatisfied with our effort to place the line in its dramatic context, claiming that they simply would prefer not to see such language in print, we can only ask, "Would you prefer that bigots who hate your group be portrayed more politely, hence more favorably, and hence more deceptively?" It is clear that as the poem stands, the more crudely the bigot is portrayed, the stronger the indictment. Is it not likely that a student subjected to this poem in a literature course would come out of his experience more sensitive to the issue of bigotry, and less willing to accept the crudities of bigots than before?

Other readers, as we have learned in various censorship hearings, will object to the profanity. But again we see that the "poem" is no more profane than it is bigoted; it is the speaker who is profane. The purist may still say that he does not want profanity presented even as part of an indictment, but I have not noticed that censorship hearings have been marked by the censors' reluctance to speak the words they object to.

Steps for the Good Censor

Though the steps we have taken so far with this poem by no means exhaust what the good teacher would want to bring out in discussing it, they show very well what the good censor will want to do before carrying out his job.

(1) He will refuse to draw any conclusions whatever from any element of a work taken out of its context. This means that he will read the whole work.

(2) He will not be satisfied with one reading. When a work is assigned and discussed in class, it receives several "readings," sometimes quite literally and always in the sense that first impressions are modified by sustained reflection. As a class progresses, a poem, play, or novel is traversed by the alert student again and again. What the censor should be interested in is what the student will get after such reflective rereading, not the errors he might fall into if he read the work without the teacher's encouragement to thoughtful rereading. But of course this means that the censor himself must go through the same process. Any censor who rejected "ug U Duh" on one reading would be a very foolish censor indeed.

(3) The true values of a work—the real moral center which we may or may not want to rule out of our children's experience—cannot usually be identified with the expressed values of any one character. What we might call the author's values, the norms according to which he places his characters' values, are always more complex

than those of any one of the characters he invents. To censor the Bible because Satan plays a prominent and sometimes even dominant and persuasive role would be absurd. It is equally absurd to censor any book for expressed values which are, for the proper reader, repudiated by the author's implied criticism.

If these three points apply to a short minor poem like "ug U Duh" they are even more applicable to the more complex reading tasks presented by long fiction.

The degree of difficulty varies, of course, depending on the reader and the work. It is easy for most readers to recognize, for example, that Mark Twain does not himself use the word "nigger" in Huckleberry Finn. "We blowed out a cylinder-head," says Huck. "Good gracious!" says Aunt Sally. "Anybody hurt?" "No'm. Killed a nigger." The whole point of this episode, coming as it does long after Huck has been forced by experience to recognize the nobility of "nigger Jim," is that even Huck cannot resist thinking as he has been taught to think. Huck here not only uses the word nigger, but reduces "niggers" to less than human standing.[4] But it is not hard—at least for a white man—to see that Mark Twain is far from making the same mistake; indeed, he would have no point in relating the episode except to show a lapse from his own values.

A Negro reader is given a more difficult task. To place the offensive word or concept into its transforming context requires a kind of dispassionate attentiveness that his own involvement with words like "nigger" may easily destroy. The word sets off responses which, though appropriate to most occasions when it is used, are totally inappropriate to the very special use that Mark Twain has made of it. It is likely that every reader sooner or later encounters books that he misreads in exactly this way. And it is highly unlikely that we will ever discover our own errors of this kind, because the very nature of our fault, with its strong emotional charge, keeps us from listening to those who might set us straight.

The Catcher as Example

With all of this as background, suppose we turn now to your objections to The Catcher in the Rye. You said that you objected to the printing of the obscene phrase that Holden tries to erase. But in the light of your objections to the book, it is surely strange to find that you and Holden have the same feelings about this phrase: you would both like to get rid of it.

> It drove me damn near crazy. I thought how Phoebe and all the other little kids would see it, and how they'd wonder what the hell it meant, and then finally some dirty kid would tell them—all cock-eyed, naturally—what it meant, and how they'd all think about it and maybe even worry about it for a couple of days. I kept wanting to kill whoever'd written it.

Holden could hardly be more strongly opposed to the phrase; it is significant, surely, that throughout the scene from which this passage is taken, the tone is entirely serious—there is none of the clowning that marks Holden's behavior in many other passages. But this immediate context cannot in itself be decisive; though it is unequivocal about Holden's serious repudiation of the phrase which you repudiate, the author after all does print the phrase and not some euphemism, and this surely suggests that he is not so seriously offended by the phrase, in itself, as you and Holden are.

Clearly we are driven to thinking about what kind of character the author has created for us, in his lost wild boy. What kind of person is it who, a moment later, concludes that his effort to wipe out the obscenities of the world is "hopeless, anyway," because they are unlimited.

You said this afternoon that you found him to be a terrible person. But supposing we begin from the other direction and ask ourselves why young readers find him, as they do (I have yet to find an exception), so entirely sympathetic. When I ask my adolescent students why they like Holden so much, they usually say, "Because he is so real" or "Because he is so honest." But it takes no very deep reading to find many additional virtues that win them to him, virtues that even you and I must admire. It is true that his honest, or rather his generally unsuccessful but valiant attempt at honesty, is striking. But a far stronger magnet for the reader's affections is his tremendous capacity for love, expressed in deeds that would do credit to a saint. The book opens, for example, with his visit, extremely distasteful to him, to the sick and aging history teacher.

Holden knows that the old man loves him and needs him, just as he needs the love of the old man; it is out of real feeling that he subjects himself to the sights and smells of age and illness. The moral sensitivity revealed in this scene is maintained through the book. Again and again Holden reveals himself—often in direct contradiction of his own claims—to be far more sensitive than most of us to the feelings of others. He "feels sorry" for all the outsiders, and he hates the big shots who, like the Headmaster, allot their attentions according to social importance and try to shut out those who are fat, pimply, poor, or corny. He has genuine affection even for the Ackleys and Stradlaters ("I sort of miss everybody I told about"), and he is extraordinarily generous, not only with his possessions (almost everything he owns is on loan to some other boy) but with himself (he is the only boy who thinks of including the impossible Ackley in the trip to the movies). Though he often hurts others, he never does so intentionally ("I was sorry as hell I'd kidded her. Some people you shouldn't kid, even if they deserve it.") His heroes are those who are able to love unselfishly—Christ, Mr. Antolini, his sister—or those who, like James Castle, show moral courage. His enemies are those who deliberately inflict pain—for example, the boys who drive Castle to suicide.

A full catalog of his virtues and good works would be unfair to the book, because it would suggest a solemn kind of sermonizing very different from the special Catcher brand of affectionate comedy. But it is important to us in talking about possible censorship of the book to see its seeming immoralities in the context of Holden's deep morality.

The virtue most pertinent to the obscene phrase is of course Holden's struggle for purity. The soiled realities of the "phony" world that surrounds him in his school and in the city are constantly contrasted in his mind with the possible ideal world that has not been plastered with obscenities. His worrying about what Stradlater has done to Jane, his fight with Stradlater, his inability to carry through with the prostitute because he "feels sorry" for her, his lecture to himself about the crudities he watches through the hotel windows, his effort to explain to Luce that promiscuity destroys love—these are all, like his effort to erase the obscenity, part of his struggle to find "a place that's nice and peaceful," a world that is "nice and white." Though he himself soils, with his fevered imagination, the pure gesture of Antolini, revealing how helplessly embedded he is in another kind of world altogether, his ideal remains something like the world of the nuns, or the world of a Christ who will not condemn even Judas to eternal damnation. He is troubled, you will remember, when one of the nuns talks about <u>Romeo and Juliet</u>, because that play "gets pretty sexy in some parts, and she was a nun and all." Nuns ought to live in the pure, sexless, sinless, trouble-free world of his ideal, just as his sister ought to live in a world unsullied by nasty scrawlings on stairway walls.

All of this—the deep Christian charity and the search for an ideal purity—is symbolized in his own mind by the desire to be a catcher in the rye. He wants to save little children from falling, even though he himself, as he comes to realize, is a child who needs to be saved. The effort to erase the words is thus an ultimate, desperate manifestation of his central motive. Though it is a futile gesture, since the world will never in this respect or any other conform fully to Holden's ideal of purity, it is produced by the very qualities in his character which make it possible for him to accept his sister's love at the end, give up his mad scheme of going west, and allow himself to be saved by love. It is clear that he is, for his sister, what she has become for him: a kind of catcher in the rye. Though he cannot protect her from knowledge of the world, though he cannot, as he would like, put her under a glass museum case and save her from the ravages of the sordid, time-bound world, he can at least offer her the love that comes naturally to him. He does so and he is saved. Which is of course why he is ecstatically happy at the end.

Now none of this is buried very deep in the novel. I've not had to probe any mystical world of symbols or literary trickery to find it out; it is all evident in the actions and words of Holden himself, and it is grasped intuitively, I have found, by most teen-age readers. Their misreadings are caused, in fact, by carrying this line too far: they often overlook Holden's deficiencies. So strong is the persuasive power of his obvious virtues (obvious to them) that they overlook his limitations of understanding and his destructive weaknesses: they take him at his word. They tend to overlook the strong and unanswerable criticism offered by his sister ("You don't like anything that's happening") and by Antolini, who tries to teach him how to grow up ("The mark of the immature man is that he wants to die nobly for a cause, while the mark of the mature man is that he wants to live humbly for one"). They also overlook the author's many subtle contrasts between what Holden says and what he does. In learning to read these and other built-in criticisms, students can learn to criticize their own immaturities. They learn that such a book has been read only when they have seen Holden's almost saint-like capacity for love and compassion in the light of his urge to destroy the world, and even himself, because it cannot live up to his dreams.

I am aware that what I have said does not "prove" that Catcher is harmless. I'm sure there are some young people who might be harmed by it, just as reading the Bible has been known to work great harm on young idealists given to fanaticism. I have not even "proved" that the book can be beneficial. Only your own reading can convince you of that; again I find myself wishing that you could reread the work with us, in class. But perhaps you will return to it now and try once more, moving from page 1 to page 277, thinking about Holden's moral life as you go.

I know I do not have to ask you (the dream continues) for your decision. As a man of honor, you can only have carried out our little experiment to the letter, and the book is now cleared of all suspicion. I should not be surprised if your experience has also made you wonder about other books you have suspected in the past.

You may have guessed by now that I have been inching my way all this while toward a repudiation of our original assumption. Is there really a place for any censorship other than the teacher's careful choice? The skill required to decide whether a work is suited for a particular teaching moment is so great that only the gifted teacher, with his knowledge of how his teaching aims relate to materials chosen for students at a given stage of development, can be trusted to exercise it.

Such a teacher can be trusted even when he chooses to teach works that reveal themselves, under the closest reading, to be immoral to the core. Let us suppose that you have performed the kind of reading I have described on a given work, say Peyton Place or one of Mickey Spillane's thrillers, and you find that it does not, as with Catcher, have any defense to offer for itself: it is immoral no matter how one looks at it. So you go to the teacher to insist that the book be removed from the reading list. You should not be surprised if the teacher replies: "Oh, yes, I quite agree with you. Peyton Place is inherently an immoral work; there are, in fact, far worse things in it than the few sexual offenses you object to. Read carelessly by high school students, it could do tremendous harm— like other books of the same kind. That's why I insist on spending some time, in my advanced sections, on this particular kind of shoddiness. I find that most of my students have read the juicier sections on their own, anyway. By placing those pornographic bits back into the shoddy context from which they have been torn, the student soon comes to treat Metalious' commercial sensationalism with the contempt it deserves."

So you see, sir (the drama has by now shifted, dream-like from manuscript to real-life drama, and I am hearty, confident, even slightly patronizing as I fling one arm across his shoulder), the only person who can conduct the fight for good literature is the person who has some chance of knowing what he is doing: the sensitive, experienced teacher. He it is who . . . .

Dreams of wish fulfillment always end with a rude awakening. My dream ends with the admission that even with the best of luck my argument about Catcher would do no more than shake a censor's confidence in his own judgment. Wide awake, I know that many censors will only scoff at any efforts we may make to reason about the issues of censorship. But as I write these final lines, in South Africa, in August 1963, I do not doubt for a moment that even an ineffectual defense of freedom is better than no defense at all.

Notes

1. As reported in The Censors and the Schools, by Jack Nelson and

Gene Roberts, Jr. (Boston, 1963), p. 136-37.

2. This phrasing was in an early draft of the excellent NCTE pamphlet, The Students' Right to Read (1962). Every teacher should own and use this pamphlet, but it does not, even in the revised form, show the censor why we misguided teachers are so thoroughly convinced that immoral books are moral books.

3. The Students' Right to Read, p. 11.

4. A possible alternative reading would see Huck as himself master of the ironies here. Since he is author of his own anecdote, he may be thought of as choosing a moral language which he knows will be convincing to his auditor. Regardless of how we read the passage, Mark Twain is clearly guiltless, even from the most passionately pro-Negro viewpoint.

"Censorship and High School Libraries" by Richard D. Gannon. Wilson Library Bulletin, 35:46-47, September, 1960. Copyright 1966 by the H. W. Wilson Company.

In our country today, censorship is used much like parliamentary procedure: a determined few always seem to learn enough of the right motions to impose their will upon others, but not enough to understand the full significance of their actions. Censorship is a reflection in and of the mind, hard to define or agree with, but existing and influencing a large part of our population. The feeling you would get after surviving an atomic war and finding a copy of Our Friend the Atom is censorship.

Censors attack when they have a chance. If you select books for your shelves carefully, justifying every book purchased, you can forget the censors. The students and parents will eventually respect your judgment; in fact, your librarianship. If a mistake or blunder is made, there will come a time when you will have to agree with the censor and remove a book, or decide to do everything in your power to prevent a book from being removed from your library. If understanding your future possible opponent will help, take the time to think out why censors attack in the first place. The whole matter is made more agonizing when you consider that a school or public library is less likely to stock books of poor taste or quality than any other place where books are kept or sold.

But censorship is not always wrong.

On the high school level, censorship is easily divided into two kinds: positive and negative (blue or orange, nice or naughty—you pick the words). Postive censorship is good, it helps a school system; negative censorship is bad, it doesn't help a school system.

Positive censorship is brought about by interested individuals or groups who are correct in demanding that a certain book be removed from the shelves. This is the kind of censorship exercised by teachers and librarians, as well as members of the book trade, who are often the first to say that certain books are not suitable for readers on the high school level. By this I mean books too easy or too hard for high school readers, books in which sex or violence is the main purpose, books of extremely poor binding, books that are dull or dated, and others, depending upon the librarian's original reasons for buying. If an improper book is put into a school collection, and this is pointed out by a student or adult, the book should be withdrawn, put on special shelves, stored, or given to faculty members or other adults who do not consider the book improper. The people who made the complaint in this case are sincere and their suggestions are valuable.

But censorship is not always right.

Negative censorship is also brought about by interested persons and groups, but with different purposes. Although the main motive is to get a book permanently removed from the shelves, these people also seek to censure those allowing the book to be put on the shelves, and almost everyone else who makes a good target. They are vocal, violent, pressure-grouped individuals who have found a cause. Saying or doing nothing is not your answer to the problems these people bring.

What frequently happens is that the librarian yields to the demands to have a book removed from his library because he is afraid of the person or group censoring. The fast, publicized attack does not give him the time to understand the situation fully or to act with deliberation. Often the librarian is forced to follow an order by an administrator, who has already assured the protester that "steps will be taken," or some other nonsense.

One aspect of censorship is almost always overlooked; an adult should have the right to buy or read anything placed before the public, but a student, not having the ability to select or pay for the books in a school library, or textbooks, must pass his right to complain to those who do have a voice in selection and buying. Adult society has the right and responsibility to control our schools; it also has the right to control the books purchased by the schools. I know there can be reasoned arguments about this, but we must face the fact that parents and other adults have the right to complain. Librarians need not be defensive. Their problems come after the complaint.

    This doesn't mean that a complaint automatically removes a book from your shelves. If the librarian agrees that the book is of poor value for students, the book is removed, without apologies, and the parent or adult is thanked for the service he has performed for the school. If the librarian feels that the complainer has a poor case, that not having the book available would deprive the students of reading matter they need, then the complainer is challenged, not with counterattack or rumor, but with dignity and firmness. The librarian is then acting as an adult, doubting the opinion of another adult. This makes the question of whether the book is good for the students the main concern.

    If two adults do not agree about the suitability of a book purchased by the school, then other adults, taxpayers, have a right to examine the book. I can't think of the best way to select a number of fair-minded people to read the book, but if all of the readers agree that the book should be removed, the librarian must also agree. If the ratio of those not wanting and those wanting the book to remain on the shelves is near two to one, then the book is left on the shelves. The minority, in this case, has as much a right to demand that the book remain on the shelves as do the majority to demand that the book be removed. If the original complaint was a direct challenge, then the effectiveness of that complaint has been reduced by the seriousness of the examination caused by the complaint.

    This procedure is not used to discourage those complaining nor to defeat their complaint; it is a device to prevent the complaint from being an attack, and to determine, honestly, whether the complaint is justified. A reasonable critic will not be offended by other adults who, after examining the matter, might agree or disagree with the original complaint.

"Two Kinds of Censorship" by Hoke Norris. The PTA Magazine, 59:10-12, March, 1965. Reprinted with the permission of The PTA Magazine.

Should we censor what adolescents read? One must begin to answer that question with an obvious admission: Whether or not we want to censor what they read, we cannot escape the practical necessity to do so. It is patently impossible to provide them with all the books published. We (or they) must select the few that time and money allow, and reject the rest. The act of selection and rejection is itself censorship, of a sort. Whether it is a benign sort depends upon how we apply it.

Our first answer, then, must be stated as a question: How can we make our censorship as harmless as possible? It can never be completely wise and right. Some books will of course be wrongly chosen or wrongly rejected, and our highest attainment will probably never be a completely satisfactory compromise among alternatives. We should begin with the realization that time is finite and therefore precious. The relatively few books that our children have time to read should be the best among the many. Why waste the quickly perishable life upon the meretricious and the factitious?

But how is one to find that best?

Many choices have been made for us (and for our children) by that impeccable literary critic, time. Time destroys bad books and preserves good books. We should begin, then, with a basic list of old books, for children of all ages. Through the years the child's library must include (to name a few) Grimm and Andersen, Milne and Twain, Stevenson and Dickens, Carroll and Baum, and, if you like, children's versions (and later adult versions) of the ancient fables and tales from mythology.

Perhaps in the early years a slight dose of Nancy Drew, and the like, will do no harm and may do good by encouraging the child to read. But in the main the child should be directed to the best, so in time he may do his own censoring. He can perform this task wisely and judiciously if, at the earliest age, he has developed a taste for the best. Our job is to make the best available to him. The likes of Nancy Drew will vanish if *Treasure Island* is about the house somewhere.

New books, I realize, present a greater problem than do old ones. Almost every publishing house has its juvenile division; we are constantly inundated with new books. Some of them, too many of them, are rubbish; a few are worthy of the child's attention. I would not attempt to make any recommendations. I would only direct the perplexed parent (and the child) to certain sources of help.

Various library and publishing journals contain reviews of children's books; these are probably available at your public library. There too you will find a children's librarian whose function it is to guide not alone children but parents attempting to guide their children. Teachers, the school librarians, *The PTA Magazine*, newspapers and other periodicals—all are available to the searching parent. There is no lack of help. Pride should not deter us from seeking it.

I realize that, so far, I may have evaded the question. "Censorship" has another meaning besides selection. In this sense it is an ugly word that implies villainous denial by force. It conjures up pictures of cops invading bookstores, judges sending authors to jail, and the hands of politician and policeman snatching books from our grasp. This kind of censorship is vastly different from the "benign" censorship we have been talking about.

Such tyranny must of course be opposed by all who cherish our freedoms. Police and politicians have no place whatever in the literary mart. They are not qualified by education, training, or instinct to reign there. When they have attempted to reign there, they have destroyed art, as they did in Red Russia and in Nazi Germany. We must preserve the right to choose our books for ourselves, and to help our children choose theirs, without interference from any censor.

Assuming that the parent preserves that right, he himself may, however, make some of the same mistakes that the would-be censors make. He may operate on the principle of rigid denial. I know of no better way to assure that a child will read a book than to forbid him to read it. Almost as certain a way is to hide it from him. If there is a book you particularly want him to read, forbid him to read it, or hide it from him, or both.

Another common mistake arises from a confused conception of what a book is. It is a literary product, not a moral preachment. The subject of the book is, in a sense, irrelevant. The deciding factor is the way in which its subject is presented. Some people fail to distinguish between the violence in the most hideous of our TV shows. They see the sex in <u>Tess of the D'Urbervilles</u> and <u>Tom Jones</u>. They do not seem to realize that it is literary judgment we are discussing and not at all moral judgment. If the literary quality of a work is high, then the morals of the matter will take care of themselves. The distinction may seem fine, or mischievous, but it is neither. It is fundamental if we are to avoid confusion, frustration, and illiteracy—and censorship.

Finally, we must remember that there is a greater problem than that of keeping an individual child from reading a particular book; it is the problem of getting him to read at all. Denial—another word for censorship—is the negative approach and therefore the wrong one. Whatever one reads, it is better that he read than not read. But of course one must not stop there. What the child reads is important too. Our job— as writers, teachers, critics, parents— is to see that he reads the best books available. Trained from the earliest years to make wise choices, he will make wise choices all his life.

"Let 'Em Read Trash" by Robert G. Mood. Elementary English, 34:444-450, November, 1957. Reprinted with the permission of the National Council of Teachers of English.

A half century and odd days ago I cut across the back lot of the parsonage grounds, went along the alley back of Baedecker's Furniture Store and Undertaking Parlor, turned into Main Street, loitered along in front of the Bon Ton Saloon in hopes of getting a glimpse of Walter Hargrove, our local junior grade Jesse James, paused to work the mud from the horse trough overflow between my bare toes, crossed the railroad tracks and arrived for my first day at school. I went rather unwillingly and with a determination that since my parents were so insistent I would go to school for a little while and then change to more important things. I could hardly have been more mistaken.

Several considerations changed my mind about school. The teacher was not the malignant hag the boys had reported her to be. The recess periods were fun, the walk to and from school was entertaining, and a lot of the classroom time was taken up with reading. I had already learned to read a little, and to excel in something after having been a clumsy, inept, and shy boy, is heady wine for any seven year old. From then on reading has been for me the fifth essence that transmuted the heavy elements of school into a precious metal. Next to the young people in my classes the finest thing about my job is that it is a job with lots of reading encouraged and even needful.

Fifty years ago the teaching of reading was in many ways inferior to the teaching of it today, but it had one or two advantages over today's. The readers (that is the books used for the teaching of reading) were less mere pedogogical instruments and more collections of selections valuable for content. And in my schools at least, there was very little prescriptive interference with children's choice of reading. There was of course much less reading material available to children then there is now, but we were free to read all there was.

No reliable statistics confirm the belief but I think there was about as great a proportion of trash in the reading material available to us then as there is today. More trash today, perhaps, but no greater proportion. And we read it all freely. Then as now some child readers read only trash and never grew to anything better. Then as now, the chief reason for this failure to read profitably was that the parents read little and that little mostly worthless stuff.

The Tip Top Weekly we bought at the railroad station newsstand was about the same sort of trash as the Roy Rogers and Gene Autry comic books except that the pictures in the 1956 stuff are colored, and a little better in draftsmanship. The Police Gazette which we read while waiting in the barber shop was about the equivalent of the magazine Male about which some reformers are so agitated. But we read freely—as our inclination turned us.

One of the lurid books we bought at the 'depot' and read, has since been issued in a three dollar edition with an introduction by J. Frank Dobie, and variant readings. Boys and girls still like it in spite of the scholarship. This is The True Story of a Texas Cowboy or Thirty Years on the Hurricane Deck of a Spanish Pony, by Charles Siringo, who lived out his last days in Caldwell, Kansas.

When, wearing out a rainy day by reading in my father's study in the church, I turned to father's edition of Swift and read the account of Gulliver's way of extinguishing the fire in the palace of the Queen Lilliput, my father's reply to my inquiry about the meaning was merely to confirm my suspicion that it meant what it said, not to suggest that I read something else. The only time I recall his advising me to avoid a book was when he found me beginning a novel called the Damnation of Theron Ware. He said "I don't believe I'd read that if I were you."

"Why?"

"I don't believe you'll find anything in it to interest you."

He was right. Not even the title (damn was tabu in our circles and sacred to the use of the preacher at revival meetings) nor the joy of forbidden fruits was enough to get me through the unvaried dullness of the book.

Problems in Adolescent Literature

At present there are several little tendencies that indicate a definite move to exercise censorship over children's books. For instance, Congressman Ed Rees of the Kansas Fourth Congressional District pushed, during the last session of Congress, a very alarming censorship bill. The activity that has recently revived my interest in thinking about the censorship of children's books is the "Better Reading Program" which the service clubs of some of our cities have sponsored. This program was the answer of the Rotary Club, Kiwanis Club, Lion's Club, and the other service clubs to the supposed menace which Dr. Frederic Wertham's book <u>Seduction of the Innocent</u> alleged to be present in comic books. When I first heard that the Rotary Club, the Optimist Club, and the others were going to censor comic books my anger rose. Actually in the program as the service clubs have conducted it, I find absolutely nothing to justify alarm, though as John Fischer points out, it is a nice boundary that divides a justifiable pressure on publication from a vicious one. The clubs have not made the slightest effort to censor children's reading. They have merely furnished to the merchants who cocoperate in the program, lists, revised frequently, of reading material which to the service club readers seems harmless. The lists include a great deal of trash and not much that is really valuable, but they are lists which the merchants can rely on as containing none of the most objectionable stuff. Curiously one of the difficulties the men in the clubs have had to overcome is that of quieting a few extremists who want to change the program to a censorship. They have overcome this difficulty.

But though this program is not censorship it has made many people think about censorship of children's reading.

To any sort of censorship there are many valid objections—objections so serious that it must be to prevent very serious injuries indeed that a censorship is exercised. With these valid objections to censorship you are quite familiar. You know that a man wise enough to be a censor is too wise to take a censor's post. You know that censorship gives an adventitious attractiveness to things that would otherwise be ignored. I am considering forbidding all of my students the reading of Karl Marx's <u>Das Kapital,</u> for I think that if I did they'd all read it, and it seems to me that the interminable wastes and dullness of that dreary work would furnish an effective life-time vaccination against communism. You all know too that there is not in history a single example of a censorship which did not make stupid blunders—blunders whose stupidity was apparent within very few years. You know that the weight of censorship nearly always falls on sincere and honest authors while sly and malicious ones easily evade it. Saintly Bishop Fenelon's work was censored; Michel de Montaigne's works, though not malicious, were much more dangerous to Catholic orthodoxy, yet they escaped almost scot-free.

It is possible, however, that the inexperience and immaturity of children so much needs protection we should risk the dangers inherent in censorship in order to protect children from worse dangers.

What dangers, we may reasonably ask?

Most present-day proposals for censorship of children's reading are directed to the comic books. The objectionable things about comic books may be taken then as the dangers to children in any reading matter. What are they? If we list the dangers and evils, eliminate the trivial ones, and the supposed evils that are really only the objections of old people to having children's lives different from their own childhoods, we still have four things which many people would eliminate from children's reading: violence and terror, incitement to misconduct or crime, banality, and sex.

In discussing these, I think we must, if our discussion is to be profitable, limit ourselves to healthy children. Children sick in mind or body doubtless should have limitations on reading as on food or play. Plum pudding is a noble dessert but we don't feed it to children who have what Al the Alligator calls "the cold Robbies." I think, however, that adults don't realize the tough-mindedness of children; the amount of violence and terror they can take without harm to themselves. The calmest, most self-possessed young mother in our neighborhood told me that between her tenth and twelfth year she read all the stories in a three-volume set of Edgar Allan Poe's <u>Stories of Terror and the Supernatural</u>, reading them by the light of a flash-light after she had been sent to bed in her back upstairs bedroom, with all the rest of her family in the living room downstairs

Problems in Adolescent Literature   143

and in the front of the house. Did the rites of the cannibals in Robinson Crusoe, the robbers in Hans Brinker, the bloodshed of Treasure Island, the devouring of the ass by the boa-constrictor in Swiss Family Robinson, the murder of Dr. Robinson in Tom Sawyer, the brimstone-and-fire appearance of Old Nick coming after the wicked blacksmith in Uncle Remus, the grisly picture of the hanged knights in Arthur Rackham's King Arthur for Boys—did these poison your childhood sleep and wreck your nervous system? As for me I read all these and Dracula and the smuggler's cave terror stories in the old Chatterbox and many more beside, and the only time I can remember having my reading interfere with sound sleep was when I read or at least looked at the pictures in Brady's Pictorial History of the Civil War, and came to the account, illustrated with pictures of the hanging of Mrs. Surrat. Perhaps even then it was not so much the terror of Mrs. Surrat's twisted neck as the fever—I broke out with measles next day.

In the story-telling sessions around the campfire at boy's camps, I always choose for telling, the bloodiest, most eerie, most mysterious stories I can command, and these for a very utilitarian reason: the boys will listen to them and so be still. And after a fifteen hour day of strenuous physical activity a boy who sits still for a half hour goes to sleep. So—in the middle of Wilkie Collins' "Terribly Strange Bed" the eight and nine year olds go to sleep, and when the story's over the big boys carry them to their cots.

But maybe this is just the laziness of the camp leaders—like the laziness of the old-fashioned Sairy Gamp nurse who'd give soothing syrup to an infant who woke at night and cried, because to do so was easier than to make the infant warm, dry, and comfortable.

And there are really valid reasons why it is unwise to shield children from all violence, terror, sorrow, and death in their reading. The way to cure a child of fear of the dark is not to deny the existence of dark, but to walk with him in the dark and show him by example the restful quiet of it, and show him too how to avoid breaking his neck by stumbling over something he can't see. Stephen Vincent Benét's story "Death in the Country" is pertinent here. It tells the story of a young couple who lived in a bright chromium-and-glass apartment in a fashionable New York apartment house where, for large sums of money, servants kept every disagreeableness away from the young people. No ugly reality entered their sleek smart world. But finally a duty call he could not ignore sent the young husband to the small town from which he'd come, to attend to the funeral of the aunt who had been his foster mother. The wife declined to go and advised him to leave everything to the undertaker, but he went, and found in the ritual and ceremony of the small-town etiquette of death a strength he had not found anywhere else. After the funeral another aunt, who survived, said to him, "I'll tell you something Tommy. When you get my age you've seen life and death. And there's just one thing about death, once you start running away from the thought of it, it runs after you. Till finally you're scared even to talk about it and, even if your best friend dies, you'll forget him as quick as you can because the Thought's always waiting. But once you make yourself turn around and look at it, it's different. Oh, you can't help the grief. But you can get a child so it isn't afraid of the dark, though if you scared it first, it'll take longer. It's not knowing that makes you scared."

Which seems more dangerous—the general dangers of censorship or the danger of too much terror and violence in reading?

Perhaps the "incitement to crime" charge against comic books and children's books in general is more serious. It is true that the newspapers have carried a good many stories about child criminals who said they gained the ideas for their crimes from comic books. If you will recall from your own childhood your own answers to your elders' "Why?" when you were caught in misdeeds I think you'll agree that the reasons children give for their crimes are seldom valid. I think it likely that the crime rate is much higher among children who read only comic books than it is among children who read better things. But isn't this merely that juvenile crime, like adult crime, is commoner among the stupid than among the intelligent? And this too, whether the juvenile (or the adult criminal) is from Snob-borough or from across the tracks. All children have antisocial impulses—criminal impulses if you will. They need no prompting from reading. But most children of normal intelligence

Problems in Adolescent Literature   145

learn, or are taught, to curb these, not alone from fear of consequence, but because they learn socially approved ways of getting what they want.

Or look at it another way. How many children do you know who have been led into misdemeanors by reading such stories of 'bad' boys as Tom Sawyer, Penrod, Jeremy, or Sube Cain. I know several boys who've wanted to try rafts on the river after reading Tom Sawyer but most of them gave up after asking and failing to get their fathers' help, and as for the one trio of brothers who got their father's help, and the hilarious help of two policemen who came to forbid and remained to help, the three boys and three adults had a wonderful time and got thoroughly wet and muddy but they never got their raft more than three blocks along the Arkansas River. Rafts need water for floating.

Books contribute very largely to children's play. The parks give a clue to what the children are reading (or seeing on television). Last week seven fifth grade boys read the Monitor and the Merimac of the Random House Landmark series and the whole neighborhood made a Monitor and a Merimac out of the firewood piled up for the barbecue pits in the Park. But no crime!

If reading about crime suggests criminal acts, we will have to suppress some very respectable books: The Bible and Shakespeare, even Silas Marner and The House of Seven Gables. True, murder by knife is treated in one way in Macbeth and in another in True Crime Comics, but neither book really promotes knifings among healthy boys.

The proposals to censor children's reading to protect children from corrupting their taste and their intelligence by reading trash, garbage, and banality, seem to me the most pausible defense of censorship. The only really valid objection to censorship for this purpose is that it won't work. You don't protect children from corrupting their musical taste by forbidding them to hear Elvis Presley—you do so by exposing them to good music.

It is my special job to foster good taste in literature by exposing young people to good books. In a garden you foster flowers by extirpating weeds, but in the mind of a young human being you don't extirpate the weeds but crowd them out, as you free a lawn from weeds by making the grass grow so lushly it starves the weeds. Did you ever notice that there are more weeds in the garden than there are in the pasture?

There remains for consideration the censorship of young people's books to eliminate objectionable presentations of sex. There is in children's books, especially certain comic books, a lot of objectionable treatment of sex. Some books designed to give children information about reproduction and copulation err in exactly the same way the army lectures on sex erred. These lectures, you may remember, told a great deal about the terrors of syphilis but very little about the bliss of a happy marriage; made much of the courtmartial penalties for fornication but very little about the compensations possible in a celibate life. Fortunately there are better things appearing on publisher's lists for children.

But I think this is not what those who'd censor sex out of children's books are talking about. They are talking about the stories and "romances" (God forgive the "logicide" or word-murder!) which titillate a secret and solitary sex excitement in the young. "Secret" and "solitary"!

Margaret Mead (Coming of Age in Samoa and other fine sociology studies) has a very fine essay on "Censorship and Sex in Contemporary Society." It is the best discussion of its subject I have read. I quote from it the conclusion to a long, serious, and objective exposition of the defensible basis of society's right to regulate books:

"It is useful to distinguish between pornographic, condemned in every society, and the bawdy, the ribald, the shared vulgarities and jokes which are the safety valves of most social systems. Pornography is a most doubtful safety valve. In extreme cases it may feed the perverted imagination of the doomed man who starts by pulling little girl's braids and ends by cutting off a little girl's head, as each increasing stimulus loses its effectiveness and must be replaced by a more extreme one. This is particularly true of the pornography primarily designed to be brooded over in secret. But it is quite otherwise with music hall jokes, and folk ribaldry at a wedding,

Problems in Adolescent Literature

the innocent smut at the smoking room where men who are perennially faithful to their wives exchange stories that lead to explosive laughter. Pornography does not lead to laughter; it leads to deadly serious pursuit of sexual satisfaction divorced from personality and from every other meaning. The uproarious laughter of the group who recognize a common dilemma—the laughter of a group of women at the story of the intractable unborn who refused to budge but only shivered under the effects of the quart of ice cream hopefully eaten by its poor mother; the laughter of a group of men at the story of the bride who asked to be "frightened" a fourth time; is the laughter of human beings who are making the best of the imperfect social arrangements within which their life here on earth is conducted, colonizers of heaven working with recognizable, imperfect equipment for the development of the human soul.

"Such laughter is the counterpoint of the good life. Shared, consecrated by usage and tradition it is an underwriting of virtue rather than an incitement to vice. Like every other kind of material which deals with the body, and especially with sex, these jokes can be misused, or labeled pornography when they are not, but the criteria of happy sharing and of laughter holds. The difference between the music hall in which a feeble carrot waves above a bowl of cauliflower while roars of laughter shake the audience of husbands and wives on the weekly outing; and the strip tease where lonely men, driven and haunted, go alone, is the difference between the paths to heaven and hell, a difference which any society obscures to its peril."

This quotation was written with adults in mind, but some of it, at least, is applicable to adolescents or even younger children. A wise school principal of a junior high school near my home broke up a sniggering smut session on the playground of his building, not by thrashing the participants, as was the custom in my day, nor by the self-important solemn humorless lecture of a decade later, but by contributing to the session a really funny malapropism made by a high school athletic trainer trying to use medical language instead of locker-room language in explaining to the mother of a boy who was injured in a game. His story brought a real lusty laugh instead of the guilty sniggers and presently the boys were back at the soccer game. It is obvious that it is no longer possible to refuse to answer a young person's questions about sex; the choice is between an honest answer and a misleading one. Even "Why don't you ask your father or your family doctor" is an answer and a partially misleading one—though it is the one I usually give.

So while I think the existing statutes against pornography should remain as the one admissible censorship, I think it even better to immunize young folks against the disease of secret and solitary brooding over sex, by giving them accurate information and by letting them use as fast as possible the adult's safety valves of shared laughter.

A story of a small town character I once knew is relevant to any thought about the supposed dangers from boys' and girls' reading—incitements to crime; shock of death, terror and violence; sex excitement—even the danger of acquiring a taste for the banal and the cheap.

The story concerns a man named Old John. His family name was an old and honorable one in the statesmanship and scholarship of the region, but he was known only as Old John. By a quirk of heredity he had been born with less mental power than others of his family. Then he had some sort of fever in his childhood which further enfeebled his brains. In his twenties he became addicted to a brew the Mexicans distilled from the sap of century plants so that when he was thirty-five he was Old John, grossly fat, dirty, and nearly imbecile. In the summers he would spend his morning with a dilapidated cart hauling trash for the few neighbors who hired him out of pity for his family. The trash delivered at the town dump, he'd spend the time till noon scavenging the dump. At noon he'd go home to eat, and after that he would come out into the yard, lower his lard-lined bulk onto a bench under the live oak tree and watch the great masses of white summer clouds float by.

These clouds are conspicuous in the summer skies all over the Central Plains. To children they suggest generous dishes of ice cream—vanilla in the afternoon, strawberry and raspberry at sunset. To the ex-Confederate colonel who had the largest farm in Old

Problems in Adolescent Literature   149

John's county, they pictured the wagons full of cotton the colonel could send to the gin if there were ever a season when sun, rain, wind, and freedom from boll weevils were just right. To some of us who were raised on Malory, Tennyson, and Canon Church's Stories from the Iliad and the Odyssey they seemed the towers of Camelot or Troy. To some they were just clouds, which to the careful observer offered clues to the kind of weather to follow. But Old John saw in them masses of fat and naked women wallowing in lewd and obscene postures. I know he saw them, for he'd describe them in detail, his little pig eyes glistening, his lips trembling, and the tobacco juice drooling out of the corners of his mouth onto the ugly stubble on his cheeks and chin.

The people of the town nearly all thought something should be done about Old John, but they differed on what. Some thought he should be sent to the North Austin Academy (so we grammar school wits called the State Hospital for the Insane). Some thought he should be jailed. Many thought his widowed mother and hardworking sister should have some relief, but no one had a very good plan. Old Pat Brady, the town marshall, thought very forcibly that we boys should not stand near the fence and listen to Old John describe his visions. But in all the various proposals about what to do about Old John, no one proposed that we should abolish the clouds, or censor them.

"The Glitter and the Gold" by Richard S. Alm, The English Journal, 44:315-322, September, 1955. Reprinted with the permission of the National Council of Teachers of English.

The last twenty years have seen not only the coming of age of the novel for the adolescent but also a flood of slick, patterned, rather inconsequential stories written to capitalize on a rapidly expanding market. Earlier, the reading available to the teen-ager was limited to literature written for adults, an occasional story of merit involving an adolescent hero or heroine, and a great many series stories patterned on the adventures or exploits of a young super hero.

Today, however, there is coming from the presses a steady stream of junior novels and novels written for adults but taken over by young readers. Writers, perhaps noting the heightened attention given to adolescents and their problems by psychologists, educators, and librarians, have turned to the personal concerns of the teenager as the focus of their novels. In the main, these authors deal with an adolescent's relationships with others his own age, with his parents and other adults, and with such worries as deciding upon and preparing for a job, "going steady," marrying, and facing the responsibilities of adulthood.

In writing about these problems, most novelists present a sugar-puff story of what adolescents should do and should believe rather than what adolescents may or will do and believe. Such stories reveal the novelists' lack of knowledge or insight into adolescent behavior as well as a lack of writing ability. These writers do not penetrate beneath the surface of the situation they create. Their stories are superficial, often distorted, sometimes completely false representations of adolescence. Instead of art, they produce artifice. They may not, it is true, intend to produce art, but they fail to breathe any life into their characters or to create stories with any substance. The reader of the inferior novel can often, from the very

Problems in Adolescent Literature   151

first page, predict with accuracy and perhaps with detail the plot, the characterization, and the outcome.

In writing for young people, the novelist is ordinarily concerned with an adolescent beset with a problem or series of problems. In the inferior novel, the teen-ager solves his problems with a minimum of effort. If he meets rebuffs, they serve only to display his exaggerated talents. He is, frequently, the all-wise person in the story, instructing and directing the adults around him. Usually he is a model of virtue—the more-than-kind, noble hero who sacrifices whatever is necessary to make others happy. The young heroine of Janet Lambert's <u>Candy Kane</u> is a classic example of such a paragon. Candy is invariably completely unselfish. When Barton protests that she does too much and suggests that the other young people in the community should reciprocate her many kindnesses, Candy says, "I like to do things for people." Jane, the young girl who works at the Officers' Club, pictures Candy as a noble influence in her life: "Whenever I'm tired or low or am thinking, oh, what's the use, you (Candy) come popping in . . . . Oh, Candy honey . . . . You're such a dear little girl."

Candy displays none of the normal reactions of a fourteen-year-old. When all her friends go to the Junior Hop, Candy is neither lonely nor unhappy. Without any feeling of jealousy or of being left out, she goes to the scene of the dance to sit on the ground outside and listen to the music. She thinks about Anne, who is inside, and wonders ". . . what Anne would say if she could see her spreading her coat on the ground beneath a pine tree, laying out a wilted bar of chocolate and a package of chewing gum. Not for all the world would she have changed places with Anne." Such saccharine sentiments are typical of this heroine who is, literally, too good to be true.

Candy's friends are voluble in their praise of her direction and advice. Dirk, for example, is delighted that Candy has resolved his problems: "I think someday you will become one of our most eminent psychologists. You snapped up both out of a complex mighty quick." At the end of the story, Candy herself summarizes her accomplishments with pride: ". . . she thought how pleasant life was.

Jane and Corp were to be married; Leigh was out with Chris; her mother and father were laughing together in the kitchen. . . . " With, presumably, the greatest of ease, Candy has settled all questions.

Oversimplification is reflected, too, in the way in which major changes in the personality of a character are quickly effected. In Helen Boylston's Sue Barton, Neighborhood Nurse, what seem to be deep-rooted problems and frustrations of the adolescent Cal are satisfactorily disposed of within eight days by the guiding angel of the neighborhood, former nurse Sue Barton Barry. In Janet Lambert's Star-Spangled Summer, an eloquent teen-ager, Penny Parrish, influences Langdon Houghton to change life-long habits of reticence to an openness and geniality that make him not only his daughter's companion and confidant but also a favorite of her new friends. The process is a simple one for Penny—writing a letter aimed directly at the man's cold heart and prescribing for him a few days' observation of what the "average American family" is like.

The motivation of such characters is reduced to a single factor. For Penny Parrish, it is her frequently expressed desire to make all others happy. For Sue Barton Barry, it is to be the all-sacrificing, perfect nurse, who, after marriage, which becomes a working partnership with her doctor husband in directing a clinic and caring for three children, still feels remiss by not being on active nursing duty.

In the inferior novel nothing is impossible for the adolescent. He sets his own goal and, armed with great determination, always reaches it. This is especially true in the so-called career stories which too frequently glamorize and misrepresent a vocation, instead of giving the young reader some real understanding of a worker on a job. For example, in the widely-read Peggy Covers the News by Emma Bugbee, young Peggy Foster prizes a job on a metropolitan daily and, despite million-to-one odds, wins one. Furthermore, though Kate Morrison, an older woman on the staff, repeatedly underscores the drudgery of a reporter's life, Peggy herself rides always on a crest of excitement. Even the assignments that would have been thought dull by other staff members fascinate her: ". . . to Peggy they were the very stuff of adventure. " She says over and over that

Problems in Adolescent Literature

hers is a thrilling job:

> This was much more fun, really, than any other job in the world. You never knew from one moment to the next what you would be doing.
>
> School teachers, poor things, always had the same old Caesar or the same old algebra, year in and year out. Librarians, saleswomen, almost all professional women did their work without much change of scene or material. Doctors, of course, lived under an always shifting schedule; but, after all, they must find measles and dyspepsia and sore throats rather monotonous, and their big adventures with victims of automobile accidents were not numerous.
>
> Peggy's mind raced along merrily, comparing her lot with that of all other unfortunate groups of wretched womanhood, doomed never to be reporters.

With little experience and a limited background but with the equanimity of a Pulitzer prize-winning by-line reporter, Peggy has established herself in the newspaper world.

Especially significant in the weakest of these novels is the writer's approach to the idea of maturity. These stories give little indication of the development of maturity, since so many of the heroes and heroines, even those fourteen and fifteen, are already performing on an adult level. They make their own plans, they work out their own destinies, they assist or direct everyone around them, including the adults.

Inconsistencies in characterization also mark the lesser adolescent novels. In Mary Wolfe Thompson's The Steadfast Heart, heroine Jo, on first meeting her foster parents, is unusually perceptive about their reactions. Later, however, she seems almost dull-witted. Even with many clues to the nature of the Bentleys' sorrow (the loss of a young son), she is, presumably, never aware of what is troubling them. Furthermore, in spite of a number of situations which pique her curiosity, she never seems curious. Although she is supposed to be primarily concerned with the improvement of the relationship between her and her sister and the Bentleys, she misses most of the opportunities to bring about such improvement.

Another inconsistency in Jo involves her status at the Bentleys and in the community. At the beginning of the story, she is embarrassed and self-conscious about being a state ward; she worries about the reactions of her classmates and of the townspeople toward her. However, in two incidents in which this embarrassment might have been heightened, she displays no feeling at all about her status. To earn spending money, she goes from door to door in town selling nuts she has gathered from the woods near the Bentleys' farm and never once is embarrassed. In the other situation, Mrs. Preston, the mother of Jo's boyfriend Marc, volunteers to write her niece for clothes for Jo; the latter is delighted and shows not the slighest discomfiture. Despite evidences of Jo's growing maturity in some respects, there is nothing in the story to prepare the reader for so great a change. Therefore, Jo is, at many points, an unconvincing character, one whose reason for being is to force consideration of such problems as dealing with a drunken father, becoming emotionally independent of others, "going steady," but as someone apart from the problem and not herself emotionally involved.

That these poorly-written stories are highly popular with young readers indicates that adolescents have little regard for the disdain or reservations of adults. Thus, these books and others like them—the series, certain sanctimonious religious stories, the patently false love story, and the monotonous, patterned Western—endure.

But not all novels written for or read widely by teen-agers are—from a literary point of view—trivial. Of those which focus on problems common to adolescents, a number are rather well-told stories about credible adolescents, working out, in credible situations, these problems. A few are works of real stature. The hero of these stories is a more complex individual whose actions are carefully motivated. He meets rebuffs, learns certain limitations about himself, develops a sense of responsibility, and makes adjustments regarding his basic problem; in short, he becomes a more mature person.

In Anne Emery, the teen-aged reader has a novelist of considerable merit. Though some of her characters may seem too <u>nice</u> and her stories too pat, she shows in her teen-agers a growing maturity, not contrived, not unexpected but rather clearly developed. Sally in <u>Senior Year</u>, for example, learns gradually that she is merely a carbon copy of the girls she chooses as her best friends and that she must learn to respect her own individuality. Sally and Scotty, in Going Steady, discover that marriage will not mean the end of their problems but the beginning of other, more complex ones. In a third novel, Sorority Girl, Emery tells the story of Jean, Sally Burnaby's younger sister, and her relationship to a high school sorority. Here Emery deals with a common enough problem but somehow is less deft in handling the situation. In none of these novels does the problem get out of hand; it serves as the focal point of the story, but the emphasis is on the characters and their reactions.

Betty Cavanna, too, is a writer of some importance. In Rette Larkin, the heroine of A Girl Can Dream, she creates a tomboy whose unconventional behavior and ambitions make her a conspicuous member of the senior class. Unfortunately, the characterization is not carefully sustained, and the story ends too neatly with all i's dotted and all t's crossed. In Going on Sixteen, an earlier story, the shy, withdrawn Julie Ferguson develops into a more self-confident, poised adolescent. This heroine is a convincing figure throughout the story. Changes in Julie are carefully prepared for and are neither abrupt nor exaggerated. The one opportunity for giving the story a fairy-tale twist—Julie's attempting to sell her sketches of puppies to an art editor to earn enough money to buy Sonny, the thoroughbred Collie—Cavanna turns instead into an experience that helps Julie to grow up. Betty Cavanna is sensitive to the happiness as well as the pain of adolescence, and her stories of teen-agers reflect both.

Another good story from a prolific writer for the teen-aged audience is Street Rod by H. Gregor Felsen. Though somewhat similar in theme to his earlier Hot Rod, this novel is a more carefully-written account of the despair of a sixteen-year-old who wants desperately to own a "souped-up" rod. The young hero, Ricky Madison, is a remarkably vivid figure in contrast to the rather superficially-drawn hero of Hot Rod. Felsen's delineation of the boy is a careful one. There is no magic alteration of his behavior; his values change slowly. Despite a growing sense of responsibility, however, Ricky finally races his rival—to his own death. This ending is a shock to the reader, not because Felsen's characterization is inconsistent but because he departs from what the typical writer for teen-agers would do in winding up the story.

A second story by Felsen which has caused a considerable stir in recent years is Two and the Town. In treating a subject which is ordinarily taboo—the pregnancy of a high school girl and a marriage forced upon two teen-agers—Felsen does an excellent job in creating plausible situations and what seem natural reactions on the part of the adolescents. The story has flaws: Buff's mother makes an abrupt about-face in her reactions toward Elaine—an unconvincing change; Buff's redemption and return to his family are too neatly accomplished to be credible. But flaws notwithstanding, Felsen tells frankly and rather well this story for teen-agers in their own idiom and with real insight into the way they sometimes become involved in complex situations which change their entire lives.

Most of the stories dealing with the adolescent's personal problems interest principally girls. Certainly of the novels which are outstanding, most are for girls. Undoubtedly, the most widely talked about and most praised of all contemporary novels for the adolescent is Maureen Daly's Seventeenth Summer. Burton believes that it "captures better than any other novel the spirit of adolescence."[1] Edwards declares that with the appearance of Seventeenth Summer in 1942 "the new field of writing for teen-agers became established. . . . This tender story of a young girl's first awakening to love bids fair to become a classic for the teen-agers as did Little Women for younger girls."[2]

Novelists themselves have recognized the significance of Seventeenth Summer. Rette, the heroine of Cavanna's A Girl Can Dream, senses what is great about the Daly novel when she reads it in preparation for a writing task of her own. "No other book that she had ever read . . . had quite the quality of Seventeenth Summer. There was a homeliness, a deep-rooted honesty, a youthfulness about it that made Loretta catch her breath. She didn't live in the sort of town Angie Morrow lived in; she didn't have the sort of family; she had yet to have a love affair. Yet the story was so real and so fresh that Rette became Angie. She shared every feeling, every im-

Problems in Adolescent Literature   157

pulse, every hope and every thrill and every disappointment."

This sense of immediacy which Rette feels in reading <u>Seventeen Summer</u> is the result of Daly's telling the story from Angie's point of view and capturing the excitement of a young girl bursting with hapiness (sic) she wants to share with intimate friends. The story is a simple one of commonplace events, day-by-day life in a small Wisconsin town; yet it is an engrossing story because the reader is able to identify himself so closely with the reactions of the heroine. What might be sensational—Lorraine's affair with Martin—is played down, and the reader's attention is drawn, not to Lorraine's affair, but to Angie's reactions toward her sister. Angie's is a superb characterization. She is introduced as a rather naive seventeen-year-old, but during one summer she learns a great deal about boys, about her own emotions, and about growing up to face new problems and decisions. That the story does not end in a Hollywood manner with Jack and Angie walking off into the sunset together is a credit to Maureen Daly who does not compromise a characterization in order to make <u>all</u> her readers happy.

In the wake of Maureen Daly but not in imitation have come other significant contributors to the field of literature for the adolescent. Mary Stolz, surely the most versatile and most skilled of that group, writes not for the masses who worship Sue Barton Barry but for the rarer adolescent who sees in Anne Armacost (<u>To Tell Your Love</u>) a girl of warmth and charm, in love unfortunately with a boy who is afraid to return her love. In a summer of endless days with a telephone which does not ring, Anne slowly understands what has driven Doug away. The poignancy of her losing this first, intense love is a bittersweet experience which makes her a little sadder, but a good deal more perceptive of the emotions and reactions of those around her.

The other characters, too, in <u>To Tell Your Love</u> are individuals, not types. In shifting her point of view from one to another and giving an intimate glimpse of the feelings and thoughts of each one, Stolz reveals a talent that few writers have. The reader can sympathize with Johnny who at fourteen wants to be husky and scorns his own long, bony frame. He enjoys Mrs. Armacost's discomfiture when her son learns the secret of her baking successes. He is impressed by the dignity of Theo's quiet romance and senses that an older Anne will probably be the same thoughtful kind of person. Stolz' other novels—In a Mirror, The Sea Gulls Woke Me, Pray Love, Remember, and Organdy Cupcakes—are significant contributions, too, to fiction for the adolescent. In all of them she tells an engrossing story but, equally important, she presents characters who emerge as sensitively-drawn individuals.

Other novels of stature with appeal especially for older girls are Mildred Walker's Winter Wheat, Rumer Godden's A Candle for St. Jude, and Marguerite Harmon Bro's Sarah. In each, the heroine faces problems of love, career, and complex relationships with others. Mildred Walker, in telling the story of Ellen Webb, gives the reader a sense of the vastness of the Montana country and of Ellen's changing perspective toward it. Her college romance with Gil ends because she feels that they, like her parents, are too different from each other ever to be happy. When he is killed in the war, however, she realizes how much she had loved him. Out of her sorrow comes a closer relationship with her parents. When Ellen says at the end of the story, "I had not always been glad that I was their child, but today I had a kind of pride in being born to them," her words reflect her new understanding of the two people whose relationship to each other had always baffled her.

Rumer Godden in A Candle for St. Jude, lifts the curtain in the theater of ballet to reveal the struggles and the glamor of the disciples of that art. Among the many facets of a beautifully-written novel is the story of a young genius almost lost in a tangle of fiery temperaments and a hierarchy of jealously-guarded positions of prestige. Hilda, earlier regarded as only a mediocre dancer, creates music and choreography which amaze even the great Mme. Holbein with their brilliance. Hilda grows up in the tradition and discipline of the art and appears destined for greatness under Mme. Holbein's direction. Rumer Godden's prose, dramatic with the excitement of the theater, serves further to distinguish this novel.

Bro's Sarah is the story of a young girl faced with the problem of choosing between two careers for which she seems to have special gifts. Despite much help and encouragement by friends who smooth her path, Sarah is nagged by self-doubts and frustrated by unrealized dreams. The fascination of the story lies in its Cinderella-like quality, but this is no pedestrian romance; Bro's skill as a storyteller makes it a superior novel.

Although there are more teen-age problem novels for girls than for boys, there are several notable stories, intended initially for adults, which have particular appeal for boys: Hie to the Hunters, The Folded Leaf, and Walk Like a Mortal. The audience for each of these, however, is limited in that the stories are not of universal interest.

Jesse Stuart, among his many accounts of the Kentucky hill people, has written a novel which focuses on an adolescent's need for independence from his family and the shift in values which such an achievement involves. In Hie to the Hunters, young Didway Hargis leaves his parents to join the hill people and comes to know a life different from his own. Later, a somewhat maturer Did returns to his own people in town, but having been accepted by the hill folk, he knows in the future he can move freely among both groups. Stuart, who as a regional writer is important on the American scene, illuminates the problems of a young boy against the background he knows so intimately. The reader gains a sense of not only the individual but also the contrast and conflict between the ways of two groups.

The Folded Leaf by William Maxwell, a novel of rare beauty, will be read primarily by the mature adolescent. In it, the author contrasts the gentle, bookish Lymie Peters and the handsome, athletic extrovert, Spud Latham. In delineating the relationship of two boys growing into manhood, he probes into their backgrounds, noting carefully the psychological influences on them. With great insight he reveals the forces which pull them together and those which eventually drive them apart. Despite the melodramatic denouement, the story is a unique study of a friendship.

In the third novel, Walk Like a Mortal, Dan Wickenden writes with rare perception the story of Gabe Mackenzie who, at seventeen, sees his parents' marriage disintegrate. Though a rather mature boy at the outset, Gabe is torn between conflicting loyalties and an inability to translate the actions of his mother and father into terms he can understand. As he adjusts to a new life without his mother, he comes to understand her better. When she returns, however, he discovers that his reliance upon her has been superseded by a more mature relationship with his father. This story of an adolescent's response to the breakup of his home is told with extraordinary skill; no contemporary writer has matched Wickenden's treatment of the subject.

Among stories read widely by teen-agers are two by outstanding contemporary writers who have heretofore been concerned with adult fiction or biography. Though not ordinarily called <u>problem novels</u> for the adolescent, The Yearling and <u>Johnny Tremain</u> do center in the development of an adolescent's personality. <u>Johnny Tremain</u>, though set in American Revolutionary days, is a timeless story. Esther Forbes writes of a teen-ager's dilemma when circumstances alter his life. As the arrogant young genius in Latham's silvershop, Johnny's future seems secure. But an accident maims his left hand and forces him to abandon his dream of becoming a silversmith. Sensitive about the appearance of his hand, scorned by his former co-workers, confused because he does not know where to turn, Johnny exists aimlessly until he meets Rab and becomes imbued with the spirit of the colonists' cause. Inspired by Rab's devotion to the Revolution, Johnny loses his self-consciousness, takes on greater responsibilities, and finally, finds for himself a part in the Revolution. Esther Forbes captures the spirit of the times and of the people. Her novel is an important social document as well as a powerful narrative.

Marjorie Kinnan Rawlings, in <u>The Yearling</u>, tells the story of Jody and his fawn, which to him represents a friend and a kind of security. Eventually, his relationship with Flag is the bridge whereby he moves from childhood to greater maturity. Rawlings writes with compassion for the Baxters who live near the soil and work desperately for a living. The reader sees Jody, growing up in an isolated spot, dependent upon an understanding father and a stern mother. Through the storyteller's omniscient eye, the reader senses the complex nature of their family relationships and the feelings they hold about each other but do not openly reveal.

Two significant stories which are concerned with a boy's closeness to nature are James Street's Goodbye, My Lady and Paul Annixter's Swiftwater. Each is a moving portrayal of a boy struggling with the world that encroaches upon his own rather limited sphere and the influence of that struggle upon him.

All the novels discussed here have one element in common: the young hero or heroine is attempting to cope with a personal problem. Each is concerned about his family or his friends or his own individuality and usually his future. Each novel concentrates, to some degree, on the question of the maturity of the central character. To distinguish between the superior and the inferior story, one must consider the novel both as a literary piece and as a vehicle for the presentation of a problem. Such questions as the following may help the reader to make such a distinction: Is the story one of credible people in a credible situation? Does the story have unique qualities, or is it a repetition of an often-used pattern? Do the characters grope somehow in dealing with their problems, or are their reactions formalized and pat? Is the problem of the adolescent in proper perspective in the novel, or does it loom so large that neither story nor characters emerge clearly? Is the stage of maturity of the central character developed naturally, a measure at a time, or is it a magic process accomplished mechanically? Is the reader given some insight into the characters' lives, or must he rely upon superficial sketches? These questions are not easy for the reader to answer, but they suggest approaches by which adolescent fiction may be more adequately (sic) judged. To the extent that a novel meets these criteria the writer reveals his ability to deal with the personal problems of an adolescent within the context of literary art.

Notes

1. Dwight L. Burton, "The Novel for the Adolescent," The English Journal, 40 (September, 1951), p. 363.
2. Margaret A. Edwards, "The Rise of Teen-Age Reading," Saturday Review, 37 (November 13, 1954), p. 88.

"The Novel for the Adolescent" by Dwight L. Burton,[1] The English Journal, 40:363-369, September, 1951. Reprinted with the permission of the National Council of Teachers of English.

"Literature for adolescents" and "adolescent literature" are terms which should not be used synonomously but often are. Novels for the adolescent reader may represent mature literary art as surely as novels for the adult reader may not. This is one prefatory remark for any discussion of novels for the adolescent. There are others. One is that when we speak of "adolescent readers" we may feel that we are talking about a very limited audience, but actually the "adolescent" or "the adolescent reader" is something only theoretical and amorphous for as every high school teacher knows the quantitative and qualitative differences in reactions to literature are as great among adolescent readers as among the general reading population. In this discussion "the adolescent" refers to a person who might usually be found in Grades IX-XII of the high school.

Perhaps it should be said, too, that the writers under discussion here have not all written specifically for the adolescent public. Several of them have aimed their work at the general public, but their writing generally or certain specific novels may have special relevance for adolescent readers. Conversely, several of the writers have chosen adolescence as their specific domain. I shall be concerned with this group first.

Maureen Daly's one novel, Seventeenth Summer, perhaps captures better than any other novel the spirit of adolescence. Probably one reason for this is that the author was so near adolescence herself when she wrote the book. In fiction with adolescent protagonists and in our thinking about the adolescent generally, we have never freed ourselves from Booth Tarkington's influence, which has projected itself into 1951 as the Corliss Archer—Henry Aldrich tradition, a vision of adolescence which infuriates the adolescent, amuses some adults, and adds nothing to the understanding of either. Seventeenth Summer is a cogent refutation of Tarkington's Seventeen. Basically, Seventeenth Summer is a serious story because adolescents, particularly seventeen-year-olds, are basically serious-minded. In simple plot the novel is the story of the love affair between Angie Morrow and Jack Duluth and their experiment in "going steady." This love is a serious, almost all-consuming kind of love, and this is important because adolescents can be serious about love, as the engagement rings on the fingers of high school girls affirm. The love between Angie and Jack has its erotic aspects, and this, too, is healthy. Many writers have been loath to admit the eroticism in adolescent relations.

In the magnificently conceived ending of the book, Angie, because of her summer love affair, gains a flash of insight into life. We are not left with the tacit promise that Angie and Jack will some day, despite separation, marry and live happily ever after. The fact that the book is written in the first person adds impact through giving the reader the impression that he is peeping into a high school girl's secret diary.

More than just a love story of two adolescents, Seventeenth Summer, with its introspection and fine mastery of the scene, portrays the adolescent validly in several of his important relationships— with his family, with his age mates, and, very important, with himself. In each of these three aspects, Miss Daly is discerning.

Paul Annixter, whose Swiftwater appeared last year, gives promise of possible interesting things to come. The author's experience in the wilderness gives him the ability to communicate a feeling for the beauty of wild places. Like The Yearling, Swiftwater presents through its main characters, Cam Calloway and his son Bucky, a compromise between a Thoreau-like attitude toward nature and the exigencies of present-day living. Cam is killed in refusing to make this compromise, and it is for Bucky to consummate it. Interwoven with this is the theme of a boy growing up. When Cam is injured, Bucky takes over the winter trap line, and his battle one day with the dreaded wolverine is the best scene in the book. The scene is brilliant for its action and suspense alone. But, more than that, it is a symbol of the rendezvous with evil which is the legacy of every adolescent who faces life squarely, the theme with which, for example, Sherwood Anderson was concerned in "I Want To Know Why." It is in this type of thing, especially, that Annixter shows promise. The author experiments, too, with the much-used symbol of the wild goose and its haunting call and attempts to provide with it a sort of unity for the novel. Cam's notion that "a man's soul could vault straight to the high hereafter on a wild goose's call" suggests the general meaning of the symbolism. Like Maureen Daly, Annixter presents an adolescent who is introspective, serious-minded, and believable. And, like Daly again, Annixter is interested in his protagonist's relationships with his family, his peers, and himself. The love plot which the author apparently feels obliged to introduce seems to be the flaw of the book. It is unnecessary except to emphasize Bucky's growth to maturity, which we would be aware of anyway.

Books by Betty Cavanna have been among the most popular with young high school readers. Her principal characters are adolescent girls, her setting is the environs of Philadelphia, and her theme usually is the struggle of an adolescent girl to gain self-confidence. Of her five or six novels, one, Going on Sixteen, is noteworthy. The others are neither better nor worse than the dozens of innocuous girls' stories which have flowed from the press in recent years.

Going on Sixteen is compounded of the humdrum in adolescent life. It rests upon its genuineness and sincerity rather than upon melodrama. Julie, the heroine, is a somewhat shy, nondescript girl who lives on a farm with her father and commutes to the town high school by bus. The story carries her through three years of high school to a point where she has apparently "found herself." The theme of the novel, although familiar, is handled well. The author avoids the easy assumptions present in many books with a similar theme, including others by herself. Boys, though they have a place in Julie's life, are not the magic medium through which she suddenly blossoms. Julie does not go to the prom with the football captain or with any "dreamy" new boy who moves to town; nor does any aunt come to visit who teaches Julie how to dress and change her personality. Julie does not blossom at all; there is no metamorphosis, but there is realistic evolution of character brought about by Julie's own efforts and recognition of her faults and by the sympathetic guidance of a teacher.

Miss Cavanna's principal general strength lies in the perception with which she presents adolescents together. Her best scenes, notably in Spring Comes Riding and Going on Sixteen, are those in which groups of adolescents are at dances, movies, or in drugstores, situations in which the unique social mores and conventions of adolescence are in operation. In Going on Sixteen the freshman dance scene is a bit of rare artistry.

Miss Cavanna is weakest perhaps in her treatment of family relations and in characterization. Her fathers and mothers, except in Going on Sixteen, where the father is a well-drawn individual, run to stereotypes. The mothers are young, attractive, and laden with patient wisdom; the fathers are intelligent, somewhat indulgent, and in a state of mild frustration with their daughters, who wheedle them. Real family problems do not exist. Miss Cavanna is inclined to categorize her characters and then proceed to the business of the story. This is a common fault; few writers for adolescents are skilful in character portrayal. Apparently, they feel either that the adolescent personality is not complex or that in books for adolescents all must be sacrificed for plot; neither generalization is valid. It is difficult to create a really believable adolescent in fiction, because in personality the adolescent, even more than the adult, is now one thing and now another.

No discussion of novels for adolescents could ignore John R. Tunis, whose name is a legend with thousands of young readers. Tunis writes of sports, and he does so thrillingly and authentically; any writer who can do this is assured of a vast adolescent audience. A great contribution of Tunis, whose success has inspired a host of imitators, is that he has conquered the sports pulp and weaned from it the great population of sports-obsessed adolescents.

Another attribute of Tunis is at once obvious. He is consistently and frankly didactic. He promotes a broad liberalism based upon his own conception of the American Dream. In All-American and Yea! Wildcats! he deals with the race issue. A City for Lincoln begins on the basketball court but quickly becomes the story of a liberal young coach's campaign for mayor against the vested interests of the town. Frequently, Tunis' didacticism is restricted to the moral sphere, as in World Series, when the young baseball player, who does not smoke, refuses a large sum of money offered him for a cigarette testimonial. Yet Tunis' didacticism is much more important to him than to his readers; he is widely read in spite of it rather than because of it. As soon as Tunis gets away from the diamond or tennis court his appeal wanes. It is revealing that A City for Lincoln, his most didactic book, is also his least popular book.

Tunis believes in the basic goodness of people. There are few villains in his stories, although the "big shot"—in sports or in politics—occasionally is one. Tunis invests his heroes with the Lincolnian traits of courage, honesty, humility, and loyalty; and, although he accentuates these traits and convincingly humanizes some of his sports heroes, there are few finely drawn characters in his novels. It often is enough that one player is the wise and aging veteran and another the raw rookie from the bush league. Tunis' plots are repetitious and commonplace, but they feature human disappointments and failures as well as success and invariable final victory.

Tunis is at his best in the baseball stories about the Brooklyn Dodgers. He knows major league baseball thoroughly, and his great flair for detail in page after page of play-by-play is his forte. That he can write exciting and authentic sports stories remains the most important thing to be said of him.

A good transition from those writers who address themselves expressly to adolescents and those who write for the general public is provided by Madeleine L'Engle, who has written for both groups. Her first novel, The Small Rain, was written for adults, her publishers tell us, and the second, And Both Were Young, for adolescents. Hence, And Both Were Young, which is remarkably similar in plot and setting to the earlier book, emerges as a sort of watered-down version of The Small Rain.

The theme of both novels is the struggle for happiness of a lonely, introverted young girl. Both girls are successful, one definitely and the other tentatively, one through winning a ski contest and the affections of a boy and the other through a painful process of trial and error. The author's recognition that adolescents, too, can be individualistic is refreshing.

Miss L'Engle's tremendous sensitivity, reminiscent of Katherine Mansfield and marked especially in The Small Rain, is her most impressive trait. She probes emotions deeply and truly. In The Small Rain there is much of the vague, disturbed pondering of people, death, and religion so characteristic of late adolescence. The rarefied atmosphere of Miss L'Engle's novels will be a barrier to unsophisticated adolescent readers.

I have chosen to discuss four writers whose work is designed for the general adult public. Two of these, Dan Wickenden, and Ruth Moore, have shown, each in one novel especially, a keen perception of the adolescent experience. It would be exciting to believe that these writers will deal expressly with themes of adolescent life in further books. The remaining two authors, C.S. Forester and Thomas Wolfe (certain apologies to follow!), both have a peculiar appeal to certain elements of the adolescent reading public.

In Walk like a Mortal, Dan Wickenden treats the urgent problem of the broken home and an adolescent boy caught between unhappy parents. Against this backdrop, the theme of the boy maturing and forming ideas of values is developed. Gabe McKenzie, the protagonist, who is a senior in high school, is vividly drawn, neither caricatured nor oversimplified. The progress of his thinking provides unity in the rather ruminative, leisurely paced story. Most books for adolescents end happily, but the final achievement in Gabe of a sense of well-being has a mature artistry unusual in the treatment of the adolescent-finds-happiness theme. Like most lucid novelists of adolescence, the author is concerned with the tripolar nature of adolescent relationships involving family, peers, and the adolescent himself.

Wickenden has established himself as a mature novelist of American family life, and Walk like a Mortal is evidence of the validity of his reputation. Not only is Gabe a credible character, but his parents and the members of his uncle's family are real people as well. Gabe's mother is not the well-balanced paragon of quiet love and wisdom of many novels for the young; she swears, she is full of doubts and conflicts, and she is somewhat neurotic generally. Gabe's father is a colorless, mediocre person. In Gabe's uncle's household, Wickenden creates a charming family circle without being trite and provides a contrast to Gabe's unhappy home. The author is interested in the people with whom his hero comes in contact as people and as individuals and not merely as necessary stage properties to be arranged brusquely in the first chapter or two.

What has been said already implies a general attribute of Wickenden—imagination. In Walk like a Mortal, there is real invention and imagination, and this is important even in scenes of student councils and high school cafeterias. With more novels specifically of adolescent experience, Wickenden could do a real service for literature for adolescents; for as James Gray says, "He has examined the 'perilous stuff that weighs upon the heart' of the adolescent with much more discernment and honesty than Tarkington ever achieved."[2]

Much of what has been said of Wickenden's novel could also be said of The Fire Balloon by Ruth Moore. Both novels reveal a true imagination, but The Fire Balloon is more an adventure in suspense and bold action which skirts the fringe of melodrama and carries a great impact. The novel is set in a Maine fishing village, and there is an elaborate attempt to portray a "type" of people. This attempt, although reasonably successful, is not important to the book; but the plot involving the young (not adolescent) fisherman provides a good deal of the suspenseful action.

There are at least five separate strands of plot. Two of these deal with the experience of adolescents; the themes are important to the transition from adolescence to adulthood and show an exciting depth of insight on the part of the author. One of the plots involves an eighteen-year-old girl's love affair with a truck driver whom she meets while working as a waitress in a cafe. To the girl the truck driver represents the glamorous world outside her somber little town and her hardworking family. But the truck driver is a transient adventurer, who leaves at the end of the summer after promising to go away with her. The rallying-together of the family when the girl is accused of stealing a car and thought to be pregnant by townsmen furnishes one of the finest touches of feeling in the book. Because of her experience, the girl finally has some understanding of the calm acceptance of a certain pattern of life by her family.

The key character in the other plot involving adolescent experience is a seventeen-year-old boy whose best friend is the son of the rich summer-colony family that the boy works for. He is bewildered by the gap widening between his friend and himself. Finally, in a scene in which the friend's father offers him a job as chauffer, he understands the barrier between himself and the rich boy. The kind of realization of both the principal adolescent characters in the novel is important to growth to maturity. The Fire Balloon touches significant fibers of adolescent experience in a moving story.

In the field of virile, suspenseful fiction, shorn of most of the improbability and falseness of run-of-the-mill melodrama, the prolific C. S. Forester has a great deal to offer. His appeal to the adolescent reader is explained largely by his zest for action, which the young reader shares. Forester is not a Conrad, but he is a good writer of sea stories. He is at his best in the Hornblower novels, which take place in the Napoleonic period when England sought to bring down the French empire. The authenticity or lack of it of Forester's historical backgrounds, prominent in all his books, is unimportant. What is important, at least to the young reader, is the tremendous suspense and action. In Lord Hornblower the great seaman is saved from death on the last page, and in Ship of the Line the captain surrenders on the last page.

The creation of Hornblower is an accomplishment in imagination. He remains consistently a human and complex character through an entire series of novels. A creature of the Tolstoyan military officer tradition, Hornblower cherishes his own definite code of ethics, which treats tolerantly of an affair with someone else's wife but will not admit of cheating a fellow-officer at cards. Hornblower is assailed by human doubts and is prey to human weaknesses; he is among other things, guilty of adultery; he is vain; he is arrogant.

Yet, in Hornblower, Forester stresses some of the most positive traits of the human personality. Chiefly, Hornblower exemplifies courage and discipline, qualities which Forester celebrates in every one of his novels. When Forester parts company with Hornblower, as he does in The Ship, To the Indies, and Sky and Forest, his talent and appeal diminish. Like most prolific writers, Forester is uneven, and he can descend to something as incredibly bad as Sky and Forest, in which we have a noble savage whose jungle kingdom is despoiled by the white imperialists. In all Forester's books there is a suggestion of Jack London and his survival-of-the-fittest theme. Men survive by strength and brain, and men are pitted not only against men but against nature—the storm, the sea, the jungle.

Mention of Thomas Wolfe in this connection is done with some trepidation. Since, as one writer pointed out, Wolfe is the kind of author who inspires invective or lyricism, his admirers may squirm at his being included in a discussion of novelists important to adolescents, while his sterner critics might chortle that this is just his niche! I take refuge in what was said at the beginning, that the range in reactions to literature is tremendous among adolescents. There are older adolescents upon whom Wolfe's novels, particularly Of Time and the River and You Can't Go Home Again, have such impact as to make the North Carolina prose-poet almost the center of a cult. Wolfe seems to be particularly the novelist of the eighteen-to-thirty age group. The remark is attributed to Alfred Kazin that Wolfe "expanded his boyhood into a lifetime." This may have something to do with explaining Wolfe's impact upon some young readers.

Wolfe's critics have been bothered by his technical deficiencies, which are quite excusable to the adolescent reader, who is fascinated with the writer's volcanic evocation of the promise of America. Wolfe explores with Whitmanesque gusto the puzzles of life, the nebulous Weltschmerz which often hangs upon the older adolescent who can and does think. The great cry of Thomas Wolfe reaches to the heart of the sensitive older adolescent as no other writer is able to do.

The good novel for the adolescent reader has attributes no different from any good novel. It must be technically masterful, and it must present a significant synthesis of human experience. Because of the nature of adolescence itself, the good novel for the adolescent should be full in true invention and imagination. It must free itself of Pollyannism or the Tarkington—Henry Aldrich—Corliss Archer tradition and maintain a clear vision of the adolescent as a person of complexity, individuality, and dignity. The novel for the adolescent presents a ready field for the mature artist.

Notes

1. Then assistant professor and chairman, Department of Language Arts, University of Minnesota High School.

2. "Emotionally Undernourished Household," Saturday Review of Literature, XXXI (May 15, 1948), p. 18.

"Let the Lower Lights Be Burning" by Margaret A. Edwards, The English Journal, 46:461-469, 474, November, 1957. Reprinted with the permission of the National Council of Teachers of English.

From where most teachers and librarians sit, Longfellow's village blacksmith is a man to envy. In the first place his finances are in order:

> He looks the whole world in the face,
> For he owes not any man.

But more than that he can lay out his work and measure his success:

> Each morning sees some task begin,
> Each evening sees it close;
> Something attempted, something done,
> Has earned a night's repose.

He can heat a horseshoe red hot, hammer it into shape, nail it to the horse's hoof and his task is done, while we who deal with the minds of young people never really know when we have accomplished what we are attempting and when we have earned a night's repose, for there is often no way to measure our performance. To work with intangibles is both baffling and exciting. Does the "Ode to a Skylark" really mean anything to the students who read it? Does the inarticulate girl sitting far back in the room fly with the bird or is she thinking of a problem at home? How many of us have been brought up short when a former student who meets us ten years after graduation asks, "Do you remember what you said one day about Caesar's feeling for Vercingetorix?" Of course, we do not remember, and we are amazed to learn that a chance remark of ours set up a train of thought in the boy's mind that changed the course of his life. If a chance remark can have such an effect, how much more power is stored in the ordered contents of books! These well-organized, carefully-wrought volumes written by great authors are literary atom bombs capable of destroying stupidity, cant, prejudice, and war itself, if they are read by the right people at the right time. The

Problems in Adolescent Literature

trouble is that not enough people read books at any time, and so the ideas in books, like our supply of atom bombs, are stockpiled.

In 1956 in the cities of over 300,000 population in the United States, the average number of books read per capita was 4.15. Of course, that is not the whole reading picture. Some people belong to book clubs, others borrow books from lending libraries and school libraries. However, these figures are an indication that as far as adults are concerned, the big ideas in books were not generally disseminated in 1956. From two to three of the 4.15 per capita circulated from large libraries were read by children and teen-agers, and many of the other titles borrowed were books of straight information or light reading. The great classics, the writings of philosophers, historians, and memorable figures fired few adult minds last year in cities of over 300,000. Since these cities provide for better library service than smaller towns and the rural districts of the nation, it is quite likely that the further one investigates, the darker the picture will become.

This problem of a large non-reading public is serious. How can a democracy keep vigorous and active when its people get their ideas from TV comedians, the neighbors, and social clubs of their communities? If democracy is to endure, we must keep alive our cultural heritage—we must make use of the wisdom in books.

In the not-too-distant past, we believed that education should produce scholars—that association with only the best literature would engender a love of only the best; that great classics studied carefully would establish taste and interest young people in learning more of the faults and foibles, the passions and struggles of people as portrayed in literature. This belief springs from our European heritage which has as its basis the idea that education was for the scholar. That it has not produced a large reading public may not be the fault of the method but of the place and the times. Millions of the adults living in 1956 had a thorough grounding in Silas Marner, Ivanhoe, The Tale of Two Cities, and maybe Henry Esmond in school. In the public library they were offered the classics and their voluntary reading was carefully selected from the "best"; yet when they read on their own as adult citizens of this republic in

1956, they absorbed on an average about one or two worthwhile books a year.

Here again, the village blacksmith enters the picture to make us sigh for the tangible hammer and the hard anvil, for in studying the reading problem, one cannot be sure where to place the blame for this situation. It may be that the one or two books the adult did read were read only because he had been trained in the classical tradition. It may be that any method of reading guidance is doomed to failure by the speed and complexity of modern living; but of one thing we can be sure: whatever we have done in the past has not produced enough readers. New methods when tried may fail, too, but, at least, new approaches might be considered and given a fair trial. This paper is an attempt to discuss the role of teen-age literature in arousing interest in reading.

In the December 1956 number of The English Journal Frank G. Jennings, in his article, "Literature for Adolescents—Pap or Protein," takes a dim view of this field, and many teachers and librarians agree with him. Is the teen-age literature as bad as Mr. Jennings believes it is? If not, on what grounds can we defend it?

The "opposition" believes that the school or public library can make good use of teen-age novels: (1) to teach the apathetic the love of reading; (2) to satisfy some of the adolescent's emotional and psychological needs; (3) to throw light on the problems of adolescence; (4) to explore the teen-ager's relationship to his community; (5) to lead to adult reading.

To Teach the Apathetic the Love of Reading

People who read books are enigmas to some young people. They wonder why one would withdraw from the hurly-burly of the street, where he could converse with people, to go off alone with a book. These adolescents have no concern with distant places, with the interplay of character, with man's struggle with fate. The girls are interested in growing up and dating; the boys like sports, space travel, cars, adventure—whatever offers an entree to a man's world.

If a high school girl whose friends are unread speaks of going to the library because she loves to read good books, she may arouse only concern for her eccentricity, but if on the other hand, she shows her friends that she is returning Seventeenth Summer by Maureen Daly and Double Date by Rosamond Du Jardin, it is quite likely that one or more of her non-reading friends will look over these books, listen to her warm recommendations of them, and return with her to borrow them at once. Moreover, these girls will tell others about them and constantly increase the number of teen-age patrons of the library.

The teen-age boy who sees his friend carrying Eric North's Ant Men, with its strange jacket, will ask what it is about. If he has any interest in science fiction, he can't help wanting to read of the geologists who were studying weird geological formations in the interior of Australia when an earth wave enclosed them in a crater where they encountered ant men and great mantises warring with each other. Moreover, one of the ant men had extra-sensory perception! This is not as good a novel as Arthur Clarke's The Deep Range, which tells of things to come a hundred years from now when a native of Mars redesigns his life and lives under the sea, tending the whale herds which supply earth's population with much of its food. The plots of Heinlein's space stories are more restrained than those of some writers, and he has a saving sense of humor, but Del Ray, St. John, Vance, and the Norths can surely take us on flights of fancy to distant planets or out into the incredible void.

Outrageous as some of these plots sound, they are the fairy tales of this technological age, and they intrigue their readers because no one can prove they are impossible. If we had been told a quarter of a century ago that the Glen L. Martin plant would manufacture an earth satellite, or that mankind would hold in its possession the instrument of its own destruction, who would have given credence to such wild tales? The Three Musketeers and Moby Dick are better literature, but they do not lure the non-reader to make a first contact with the library.

If there is one subject dear to teen-age boys it is automobiles. All of them either own their own cars or hot rods or dream of owning them. In Felsen's Hot Rod, one of the earliest stories in the field, Bud Crayne's race with the policeman, his insolent attitude that brakes were only for sissies, and the results of his folly make a story all boys love. In Street Rod Ricky and his girl Sharon can't resist one final street race and end up in the river—dead. Don Stanford's The Red Car and Pattrick O'Connor's The Black Tiger move into the sports car field. In both there is a good story that gives the teen-age boy a feeling for MG's and Jaguars and lets him see that while they may not be as fast on an open stretch as a stock car and though they are rough to ride in, there is the feel of power— the wonderful ability to go around corners fast and all the excitement of racing. These, with Harkins' Road Race and Gault's Thunder Road, are as tempting to boys as are white-heart flies to brook trout. For younger boys who wish to read of adventure, there are many well-written stories which were analyzed ably by Dr. G. Robert Carlsen in his article, "To Sail Beyond the Sunset," in The English Journal for September 1953.

Few of the books listed above will ever be classics, but they speak to young people in language they can understand on subjects in which they are interested. For that reason, they are bait to lure reluctant readers. It is a case of "Won't you walk into my parlour, says the spider to the fly," except that the librarian's intentions are good ones. Unless one can convince the adolescent that reading is fun—that he must make a place for it in his busy life—there is no hope of ever making him into a reader. No books accomplish this so quickly for the masses of teen-agers as the teen-age novels.

To Satisfy the Adolescent's Emotional and Psychological Needs

Why does a teen-age girl rush to the telephone after school to call up the friends she saw all day and with whom she rode home on the bus this very afternoon? Why does she talk for hours and hours on the only telephone in the house? Why does she giggle so much? Why is she such a pain in the neck?

Because she wants so desperately to be popular. She must find out how to be attractive to boys before old age overtakes her. She is only five short years from twenty when old age sets in, and if she does not succeed in being alluring, she may end up as a "brain" with a job and never know the meaning of love and never have chil-

Problems in Adolescent Literature   177

dren or anything! She is beset by her own worries and fears, she is often callous to the rights and privileges of others, and indifferent to the advantages of a really good education or the charm of culture. However, in the midst of her feverish turmoil, busy as she is, she will go the library and borrow, one after the other, all the books by Du Jardin, Headley, Cavanna, Emery, Craig and other authors of what she calls "teen-age romance."

Boy Trouble, Double Date, Going Steady, Going on Sixteen, A Girl Can Dream, Lasso Your Heart, Campus Melody, etc.—to the adults fresh from reading Wordsworth's "Ode on the Intimations of Immortality" or Proust's Remembrance of Things Past, the very titles of the books are nauseous. The plots as summarized by the publishers on the book jackets also are likely to raise the blood pressure of the literati. Two sample blurbs from dust jackets are listed below:

> It ought to be the best year of all—a girl's senior year in high school, but for Sally Burnaby it got off to a bad start. Her best friend went away to boarding school; and Scotty, who used to be as dependable as a habit, suddenly started dating a new girl. . . . —(Going Steady by Anne Emery)

> Marcy is left high and dry in high school when her steady date, Steve, departs for his freshman year at college. — (A Man for Marcy by Rosamond Du Jardin)

The warmest defender of these stories would not recommend them for the Great Books list nor ask to be marooned with them on a desert island, but they have their good points. They are wholesome, they show underprivileged girls how nice girls attract boys, how they converse, how they fit into their individual family circles with respect and affection for all. They show them how to approach the problems of dating with common sense, and the Lord knows, they tell them how to dress—the charcoal skirt and green sweater, the pink shorts and white tee shirt with a little pink ribbon tied around the pony tail, "the black velveteen jumper with the scoop neck and the full, full skirt that whirled so prettily over my crinoline petticoat."

James L. Summers has mapped out for himself the field of

teen-age stories for boys, written in something of the same vein as the romances for girls. His earlier books are quite entertaining. Open Season is a collection of short stories of high school life as it is lived. Prom Trouble tells of Rodney Budlong's difficulties arranging the junior prom, and Girl Trouble begins with the dark night a high school boy is turned down by the girl he asks to go "steady" and then accidentally smashes his father's car, which he can pay for if he gives up football and gets a job. Since boys do not feel the need to concentrate on their school and lovelife as do girls, they do not read Summers' stories avidly. However, many girls like them. Unfortunately, his later books seem less related to common high school problems and their constant cleverness wearies the adult reader.

The teen-ager is just discovering the appalling fact adults know all too well—that we are all essentially lonely. He has an idea that his unformed worries and fears, as well as those clearly defined, are peculiar to him. In these simple little stories he welcomes the discovery that what he thought were his individual problems are common ones which others have faced and solved. He takes courage and makes a quicker and better adjustment when he reads that others have come through all right. There is yet another psychological factor to be noted here. The technical term for it is probably "wish fulfillment." The more awkward and shy and unglamorous a girl is, the more interest she may have in reading of a girl who is the embodiment of what she herself wishes to be. Certainly a steady diet of stories of happy people leading happy lives may dull the senses over a long period of time, but a few books of this type may be no more harmful than the child's fairy tales if the individual's reading is directed eventually to a more balanced realism.

To Throw Light on the Problems of Adolescence

Besides the problems of growing up and learning to get along with one's family and friends, other problems are dealt with in teenage fiction. In A Cup of Courage Mina Lewiton tells of a girl who discovers that her father is becoming a heavy drinker and she, her brother, and her father attempt to cope with the situation in a story that should be of help to other teen-agers with problem parents. In this same author's Divided Heart, Julie realizes that her charming, shiftless father expects her mother to support him and that eventually the two people she loves will separate and leave her desolate. In the end she discovers for herself the old truth that if one works hard at something worthwhile he can assuage grief more easily. Clarice Pont, in Sally on the Fence, also tells of a girl with divorced parents who, when her mother died, had to accept a home with her father and his family, where she had difficulty in adjusting.

Mary Stolz is a realist who writes with understanding and poignancy of the problems of maturing, as well as of the satisfaction of finding oneself. Among her characters are Anne of To Tell Your Love, who spent a summer hoping Doug Eamons would call her on the telephone and come back to see her. Teen-age girls were aghast to discover he never did call nor come back. He actually quit her and she had to get over it the best way she could with her nice family's help. Shortly after this was published, this librarian predicted a very limited audience for Miss Stolz, but she underrated the girls who came to realize that this author was writing of life as it is.

What can a girl do about an overly-possessive mother who selects her clothes, makes all her decisions, and insists on being one's best chum? (The Sea Gulls Woke Me.) Bessie Muller of In a Mirror was too fat and kept on eating because the boys didn't like her anyway. In Ready Or Not, Morgan Connor's mother was dead, her father was a timid failure, and she had to keep the family together at the age when she wanted to explore the world of dating and romance. Dody (Pray Love, Remember) escaped from her routine life and prosaic family to glamorous Oyster Bay and a rich household for whose little boy she was responsible. Strange to tell, the Oyster Bay family wasn't much better than her own, and Dody's sense of values was confused until a Jewish boy, before he died, showed her how to establish standards and measurements for life's intangibles.

Because of Madeline is a tour de force telling how a bleached blond from a decidely bourgeois background breezed through an exclusive private school, unmarked and unimpressed by her socially prominent classmates. Yet the reaction of other students to her showed Dorothy, the central character, that—though her wealthy family had given her taste, intelligence, security—she was a snob and a prig and that if she wished to become a real person she would have to get over being the "select-girl-school" type and look for merit in people beyond the fact that they are on the "accepted" list in society.

In <u>The Tall One</u>, Gene Olson has written the story of Miles Talbert, an adolescent boy over seven feet tall who could play basketball but couldn't endure the catcalls and jeers his height provoked. This fine realistic story has a great deal to say without seeming didactic. In the end, the tall boy concluded that "he didn't really have a problem at all. It was the people who made fun of him who had the problem. If it was their problem and he couldn't do anything about it, why worry about it?" What good advice this is! Many adults have been bitter and unhappy because they were never able to make these simple adjustments.

Another problem skillfully handled in teen-age fiction is that of Linda Doverman whose charming, beloved father is sent to the penitentiary for embezzlement, in Catherine Marshall's <u>Unwilling Heart</u>. Linda's initial reaction of shame, of being unable to go to the prison to see her father, of taking offence at real and imagined slights is gradually changed until, in the end, she learns that she cand do what she has to do. After sacrifice and work and worry, she could say at least, "It doesn't matter whose daughter I am, I'm me."

To Explore the Teen-ager's Relationship to His Community

One of the earliest of the realistic teen-age novels was Felsen's <u>Two and the Town</u>, which shook up conservative librarians as it dealt frankly with the problem of the high school boy and girl who were forced to get married. It wasn't any more Buff's fault than Elaine's. It just happened. The two respectable middle-class families got hold of a minister, married the children off, and sent them on a pseudo-honeymoon. The boy's resentment at being married when he might have been playing football, the girl's embarrassment at being asked by the school principal not to come back to school, the coming of the baby are skillfully handled, and though the ending holds out hope that the boy may grow up to his responsibilities, the beating the two took for a year or more would surely dismay any adolescent.

John Tunis' books were the forerunners of the teen-age novel that dealt with one's relation to his community. All-American asked in effect what the attitude of a white high school student should be when the star of the football team was barred from a district championship game because he was a Negro. Keystone Kids dealt with a Jewish player on a professional baseball team, pointing out that both the team and the Jewish teammate needed to change their attitudes.

Three more recent books have presented the Negro problem as it affects high school students. Blanton's Hold Fast to Your Dreams tells of a Negro girl who left Blossom, Alabama, with its segregation and prejudice, to live in Blue Mesa, Arizona, where her opportunities as a ballet dancer were much greater but where prejudice was still present to a degree. The problem of prejudice is presented well, but the story is weakened by a too glamorous ending. Adele De Leeuw's Barred Road is a convincing account of a white girl who attempts to stand for fair and impartial treatment of the Negroes in her high school and to maintain a friendship with the daughter of a Negro doctor. Despite the polite antagonism of school authorities, church people, and her own mother, the girl follows her conscience, but is often beset by doubts of the wisdom of her course. In the end, she decides that one has to live with himself and that if one believes in a thing, he has to work for it and fight for it whether others do or not. By preserving her integrity of purpose, she gains stature and, in the end, the respect of her friends.

Just off the press is Catherine Marshall's Julie's Heritage, which gets off to a slow start but is the moving story of Julie, a talented, attractive, well-to-do Negro girl, who had both white and Negro friends in grade school, but finds as she enters high school that race limits her associations. She is never sure whether it is better to endure slights stoically or to make an angry defense, whether to identify herself with her race or to ignore the question of face and strive for acceptance as a person in her own right. Her Negro friends solve the problem in different ways. Lorraine, an older girl, "passes"; Slim moves to another place; George accepts a pattern of defeat; and her friend Dave decides to become a lawyer and fight with the NAACP rather than fight alone. Julie, in the end, accepts herself for what she is, establishes a warm relationship with her white friends, and arrives at the place where she can take pride in her Negro heritage.

Jan Karel, in A Chance to Belong by Emma Jacobs, had problems, too. His family were D. P.'s from Czechoslovakia. His father had old world ideas of hard work and obedience to authority that complicated Jan's relationship to his school mates. A different accent, different customs, sensitivity over not being an American citizen—all are faced and contribute to growth and understanding for younger teen-agers. For older readers, Corinne Gerson's Like a Sister tells of a German teen-age girl who comes to live in the Peterson home with a typical American teen-age girl and how their different points of view make adjustments difficult.

One of the very best books in the "problem" class is Take Care of My Little Girl by Peggy Goodin. With keen satire, she writes of a smart girl's disillusionment with college sorority life. Probably the book will not prevent a girl from joining a sorority, but surely some night when she is swearing eternal sisterhood in blood or voting to blackball a Jewish girl or slavishly keeping up with the crowd, she will sense that she is being silly.

Because sport stories speak a man's language, many a boy will read them and from quite a few learn obvious truths. John Tunis realized this and undertook in his stories to bring home to boys the practical lessons of democracy. Few of his successors have tackled so lofty a theme, but they do develop some sound ideas. Robert Bowen's The Big Inning is a study in values. Lou Sanders is upset at a lie told him and is involved in an accident that ends his career as a professional ball player. Eventually, he finds himself again in a sort of Boys' Town in Texas, where he coaches a ball team made up of underprivileged boys. Later, when he has a chance to go back to professional ball, he decides to stay where he knows his work has meaning. In <u>Infield Spark,</u> the hero overcomes his fear of spikes; in <u>Fourth Out,</u> another player gets over his fear of the wall. Sometimes this author loses his restraint and slips into sensationalism, but his best stories are very good indeed.

William Cox's <u>Five Were Chosen</u> has no big lesson, but it is top-notch basketball that gives the reader a real workout. Duane Decker's baseball is so real the reader feels the hot sun on his back as he sits in the bleachers and urges the Blue Sox on to victory. In these stories the players are real people and their problems the reader's. All of them show character development. In <u>Hit and Run,</u> Chip Fiske was high tempered and in a spot where he needed to be cool, for the manager of the Blue Sox had brought him up from the minors to replace Augie Marshall, the darling of the crowds. The stands called him "Itsey Bitsey," roared for Marshall, and never gave Chip a chance. After weeks of merciless jeers, he stood one day in front of the stands waiting for the catcalls to end. But they didn't, and instead grew louder. When a pop bottle flew out of the stands and landed at his feet, he picked it up, turned around, and heaved. "Right then," Decker says, "Chip knew this was a game he'd remember for a long, long time, for as the sports newscaster said in the morning paper, 'this Fiske, who can control his bat the way a magnet controls a needle, simply can't control himself.' "

C. H. Frick's <u>Tourney Team</u> and <u>Five against the Odds</u> are fast-paced basketball stories with the themes of overcoming bitterness at one's physical handicaps and of fair play, especially for the Negro in sports. William C. Gault, in <u>Mr. Fullback,</u> writes a story of "hired" players vs. clean college football, while his <u>Mr. Quarterback</u> is concerned with a Polish boy low on funds who wins a football scholarship to a rich man's college.

The writers of sport stories are too numerous to mention. Archibald Friendlich, Leonard O'Rourke, Waldman, and many another have provided us with what the sportsmen would call "good, clean stories" of almost every sport. Before leaving the field, special

184   Adolescent Literature

mention might be made of Jack Weeks' The Hard Way. Mario Canto lived in the slums where the boys played stick ball because there wasn't room to bat a baseball. His brother was a full-fledged juvenile delinquent who allowed Mario to take the rap for him and go to the penitentiary where he learned baseball the hard way. This is a fine story for any teen-age reader, but it is one of the most effective stories in print to lure the slum-dweller and potential delinquent into the library.

To Lead to Adult Reading

Any librarian or teacher truly interested in developing readers can turn teen-agers to adult reading if some study is made of the next step in reading; i. e., the simple adult book written with warmth and understanding that further develops the themes about which the teen-ager is accustomed to read. Almost any boy who has learned that reading is fun and has the library habit will read:

    Shaw - Gentlemen, Start Your Engines
    Piersall - Fear Strikes Out
    Murphy - To Hell and Back
    Whitehead - The FBI Story
    Lockwood - Hellcats of the Sea

Girls can easily be transferred from teen-age stories to:

    Freedman - Mrs. Mike
    Buck - East Wind, West Wind
    Bronte - Jane Eyre
    Medearis - Big Doc's Girl
    Turnbull - The Rolling Years
    Dolson - We Shook the Family Tree
    Wilson - The Nine Brides and Granny Hite

There are many other titles that could be added to either list. Most of these uncomplicated, absorbing stories will lead directly to other adult books on similar subjects. Such a progression seems a better idea than to suggest that writers of teen-age books consider adult problems, as did Emma L. Patterson in her review, "The Junior Novels and How They Grew," in The English Journal for

October 1956.

Of course, with the older teen-agers who are established readers, the librarian can ignore the entire field of teen-age reading, but for younger, reluctant readers who have formed the reading habit with teen-age novels, the adult titles listed above may be the next step to voluntary, worthwhile reading.

In America, though more and more provisions are being made for the gifted student, the public schools and the public library are rightly committed to the enlightenment of the masses. If the masses are to recognize demagogues as they arise, if they are to vote as individuals instead of as city blocks under the rule of a political boss, if they are to understand the problems of this country and its role in world affairs, they need to avail themselves of the wisdom in books. Certainly teen-age novels will not solve the world's problems, but if they lead more people to a first understanding of the pleasures and profits of the printed page, they have a place in the reading program.

"Literature for Adolescents—Pap or Protein?" by Frank G. Jennings, The English Journal, 45:526-531, December, 1956. Reprinted with the permission of the National Council of Teachers of English.

The stuff of adolescent literature, for the most part, is mealy-mouthed, gutless, and pointless. "The standard thing in contemporary 'juveniles' is a formula which anybody can apply; all that is required is—well, its application. . . . The general slovenliness with which this mass of reading matter is written and printed increases even faster than the appalling rate of production; and nine-tenths of it is saturated with diction and grammar of exactly the sort that drives college teachers distracted by its obstinate persistence in undergraduate writing. " That last groaning clause is a give-away. No, this is not an indictment of the current crop of writers for the teenager. These remarks appeared twenty-seven years ago in the long dead Bookman. A Mr. Wilson Follett was viewing, with alarm, trepidation, and profound malaise, the consequences of The Rover Boys, The Outdoor Chums, The Putnam Hall Cadets, et al., ad nauseum, upon the minds and morals of those children who later matured through the Great Depression and survived the Greatest War, second phase.

It is always open season on the scribblers of juveniles. The literary almanacs for more than a hundred years have posted critical bounty upon these "varmints. " The Penny Dreadfuls sent ripples of disgust down literary spines with as much vehemence as do the horror comics today. Horatio Alger left a cloying favor (sic) on reluctant moral taste buds—but not for all, and not quite. For Mr. Follett pointed out that whatever its shortcomings, and they were admittedly many, Alger's tale "had at least the solid merit of being adventurous. Its triumph, however little 'true-to-life, ' was a triumph over enemies that are powerful, disasterous and real, in life as well as in fiction. There was, in fine, something at stake worth writing about. "

'Twas ever thus. The current crop of pap is pap-veritable, but the tomes of our youth, whatever their admitted shortcomings, were— well, they did give us something solid to hang onto. In talking over the ancient Follett article with a friend, who is a brilliant, sensitive, and successful teacher, I was told that I missed Follett's error. "Admitting all of their shortcomings, The Rover Boys, " he said, "and all the rest gave you and me a solid grounding in values that makes us—etc. " Yes, the readers of The Rover Boys have gone into the world, died on some of its battle fields, grown old enough to have teen-age children themselves, and have even learned to vote the cautious slate.

The Book World of Youth

Is this what the harvest of our criticism must come to? Must we cluck with precocious senility over the literary food of our young, the while we measure it against the memory-enriched fare of our own forgotten youth? I think not, though it is a caution to be observed. For one fact stands out even in the mistreated evidence I have so far offered; we do a cleaner, clearer job of writing than was done for us. Most current teen-age fiction, whatever its other many shortcomings, has a familiarity, an easy control over the mechanics, at least, of our language that was hard to come by a generation ago. For this our writers deserve a cool place in hell—but for the rest, for content, for style, for thought, for consequential plot, for the quality of character development—how fares the book world of youth?

The writers for children of all ages talk down to or at but seldom with their audiences, but this is an antique failing. If there are other excellences, this can be forgiven. But only up to a point. It is a very ticklish business, this writing for the young and those who try, however small their success, at least merit our approbation. It is true, as some cynics observe, that "kids will read almost anything. " It is equally true that they won't try very hard to read anything. This is especially so for the TV and comic book incubated little minds—they are, in David Reisman's excellent and dangerous phrase, the most passive of our consumers. Yet this is really an indictment-cliché. The mass media are not the cause although they may be the contributing factor—if the laity are not looking, I'd like to hint that we start the erosion in the schools. Take a look at the primers—set aside for a moment the peculiar problems they are designed to cope with—consider the content of any one of them; consider the diction, too. Is it any wonder that a six-year-old laughed himself to sleep over "Look, Jack, look. See the ball. See Jane with the ball . . . etc. " He called it a silly book. He was right. Is it really necessary, even considering the attendant problems, to insult the child's intelligence at the very beginning of his reading experience? Is it required of us that we make of this insult a continuing ritual throughout the whole of the school career?

I am not moved or impressed by the responses that are so easily elicited from children that "This is a good book, " "We really like this one, " etc. This is the result of a cheap-jack selling job that any adult can put over. "Take his money my son, praising Allah, the kid was ordained to be sold. " The teacher in the classroom can make a strong magic. She can make a very dull story come alive. She can generate out of her great love for children an atmosphere of excited reality far beyond the scope of the paltry material with which she deals. For this, may she be blessed with tiny prayers.

It may be asking far too much that we take literally all of our own pious talk about respecting the child's intelligence, of meeting him "where he is, " of dealing fairly with what he finds important. But just because, at the beginning of reading, he must use a vocabulary that is almost devoid of the sophistication that his spoken language possesses, is it really fair to him and to what he might become to treat him like the baby he has long since ceased to be? I am tempted to accept the trap that Follett has wound up. The ancient moralistic primers with their thick crusts of adult wisdom had at least the virtue of taking the child seriously, if not lovingly. The need of all children is to be taken seriously. But throughout the pages of far too many of the textbooks, still in use and still being written, is the attitude that ideas of any consequence must be pre-digested, their toughness broken down before they are palatable to the young. The consequences do not appear to be very terrible

Problems in Adolescent Literature 189

in the early years, but by the sixth grade, the foreclosures begin. "The social studies book is boring." "The English reader has a couple of good stories but most of them are boring." "Gee, science is real stupid." "The math problems are crazy. If I wanted to know how old someone was, I'd ask them."

Of course these comments are not general; if they were perhaps something would have been done a long time ago. But such comments provide indexes of the depth and gravity of the situation. The surest source of boredom, the most certain path to the perdition of distaste in reading, is the classroom book. And if the child gets no help at home, which is probable, if the library doesn't happen to him, as it doesn't to most children, he will begin to look forward to the end of schooling as a release from the tyranny of the printed page. Fortunately there is a knight in rusty armour waiting in the wings on a phony horse—or maybe he is a clown or a tout. At any rate, he is the author of books avowedly directed to the kids. He is the grandson of Alger, the child of the Rover Boys, a cousin, twice removed, of Jack London, and he loves animals. And yet while we must be thankful for small favors, it is about time that we became a little unreasonable.

Ever since the writing of "juveniles" has become a commonplace practice among the writing fraternity, there has been a tendency to accept the product with only the most superficial of criticism. It will hardly be news to anyone who has managed to keep up with the general output to learn that much of it is really third-rate, that little of what is written for the children is one whit better than what gets into the classroom reader. The complaint of Follett still haunts us. And, though we have miraculously escaped some of the dire consequences that he predicted, the facts of the case are still unpalatable. If we respect the child as much as we claim to, and even this is to be questioned in some quarters and in some practice, then we as teachers should assume a far more active role than we have as critics of contemporary writing for children. The need for a creative, constructive criticism is nowhere so apparent as in the field of books for the teen-ager. It is not necessary to quote title and author; they can be filled in by any teacher or librarian who has even flipped the pages.

Types of Juvenile Fiction

Consider first of all the "career book," designed to fill a "felt need." Now granting the use of the book as an excellent vehicle with which to introduce the young person to the world of work and ideas, is it really enough to hang upon the very bare bones of a vocational guidance outline the stringy, dehydrated flesh of a story that would be shunned by the soap operas? Can we afford to abide the parading of two-dimensional cut-outs, masquerading as characters in the "story." Can we suffer the children to be exposed to a shill-game plot where everything happens as it never really does? Is it really permissible that an occupation or a profession be portrayed in a tinsel fashion that Hollywood, in its palmiest days, would have avoided? What is the purpose for which these books are written anyway? If it is essentially to introduce the young people to the way of the world in this particular enterprise, cannot we at least have believable characters, suffering through events to knowledge and control? Is there a place, really, for this kind of make-believe at all? Can't we do better with some honest reporting, some simple straightforward biographical writing about people who do work, who have gained success or skill or both? The career book at its best is a patent phony; at its worst it is an incontestable bore.

There is an old chestnut in the trade that you can't go wrong with an "animal story." Give a boy or girl a horse or dog to love, put the dear, brave creature through some agonizing situations, and you have it made for half a dozen volumes. The prototypes are Black Beauty and Buck and White Fang—how far wrong can you go? Just look at the record of achievement and descent. It is true enough that the boy or girl in the "animal book stage" doesn't ask for very much. This is hardly reason to give them so little. There are tastes to be developed here and discriminations to be sharpened. Here, too, is where the values that are basic to our way of life are to be spelled out with less equivocation than they ever can be again. But they need defense, not mere declaration. Honesty, loyalty, truth-seeking, responsibility, fortitude, and all the host of vibrant values

Problems in Adolescent Literature   191

need to be set forth with more royalty, more sovereignty. They are not "things" that just happen to "good" people. It is their acquisition that makes goodness. And they do not come as easily, as cheaply, as the professional lovers of our four-footed friends say they do. How can a youngster really evaluate character, the personality of a human being in a human situation, if he has learned to expect that the source of values is a kind of cosmic slot-machine guarded by the Houyhnhnms.

A very strong second to the animal book is the "mystery." These usually run in packs, in exhausting series with one common central character, boy or girl, of indefatigable resource, good and kind to a fault, who faces bank robbers, kidnappers, assorted thieves, and agents of dark unnamed powers. The formula is worked up with cookie-cutter precision—once—and ever after used with the creative skill of an antique mimeograph machine. (That boys and girls do read these things is evidence incontrovertible that they do want to read and like to read well enough to put up with the most fantastic obstacles.)

Then there is the "love story." With the support of most of the human sciences, with the treasure house of our literary heritage, with the record of magical achievement in every language, from every place and time, with all of this and the songs of all young lovers, we deal up confections of the No-Cal stamp. But perhaps teen-agers in love are really as dreadful and as frightening and as "disgusting" as some teachers seem to think; perhaps we need those writers to help us pull the fangs of love. Sex never rears its curly head in these antiseptic volumes. Body chemistry is suspended, and personality friction is lubricated out of existence with the sweet syrup of ersatz "teen-talk" of dates and dances, and faint-hearted misunderstandings—between father and son, mother and daughter, or the other possible combinations of confusion. And all of this happens only to the clean-limbed, the well-bred, the comfortably-housed-and-clothed middle class miss and boyfriend.

Over-Protection in Junior Books

Certainly, it is one of America's great virtues that it really strives toward a classless society, and sometimes even acts as if it were one. There is plenty of evidence from the social psychologists that we all like to think, in certain circumstances, that we are members of the great monolithic middle class. Teachers, by profession, are card-carrying members of the middle class. It is true that the middle class virtues are the ones to be defended. They are unquestionably the most viable, the most socially effective, and ultimately the most democratic of all virtues. But they cannot be merely paraded; they must be sold, sold upon the basis, not of the hucksters' cant, but upon the sound argument of practice. Teen-age love is the testing ground and the trying-time. Everyone gets hurt a little bit, but clarifying failure is always present. Here is where we really begin to learn to live with others and with ourselves. Here is where all of the other things that we have been beginning to learn slowly begin to shape up, to fit into place, to gather collective meanings—here is where life adventure begins to present itself at a closer horizon. But it is dangerous and frightening—so—the boys will line up at one wall, the music will begin to wail, a few girls will gather and titter and —sugar-plums, sweetpeas, and blue-suede shoes. . . .

There are other categories on which this complaint can be fixed; the adventure story, the rewritten, i. e., emasculated classic, the disemboweled myth and folk tale, the quasi-historical novel, the "simplified" biography. All of them may be labors of love. None of them betrays even a modicum of respect for the intelligence of the young people. They want more than this. They deserve better and they get better writing on their own. There is, as any teacher knows or can find out, a veritable "underground library" that exists in most secondary schools. These are the books that are circulated, without benefit of adult sanction; in fact, they circulate in most instances specifically because of adult disapproval. They are the paper-covered reprints of contemporary hard-boiled fiction as well as quite a raft of really excellent adult fiction. There are always several titles that get the widest circulation precisely because when discovered they are the ones that elicit the loudest condemnation from the teaching staff.

Here is an anomalous situation. Teachers claim, with considerable honesty, that they are dedicated to the proposition that the child develops into the thinking, reading, discriminating adult. When the teen-ager, especially, tries to taste the strong meat of a solidly-written book, the teacher is terrified—of exactly what, it is hard to say: the censure of the parents; the fear of the administration; the criticism of some value-freezing community pressure group; or perhaps the teacher's fear of his own competence in dealing with full-bodied human situations?

It is obvious, of course, that some of the reasons that bring the boys and girls to these books lie in crude, vulgar animal drives, but for all that, they are not illegitimate. Despite the initial "charge" that the readers may get out of specific references to certain facts and situations with which they already have at least a second-hand familiarity, they almost always become involved in the heart of the matter. In their reading they can go on to the richer, fuller-dimensioned aspects of plot and character development. It is not being suggested that what they are reading here is by definition great literature or even good writing, although both are better represented than in the carefully culled material found on most school library shelves. Here are young people, trembling on the threshold of adulthood. They want to know what it is like to hope and fail, to suffer, to die, to love wastefully. They want to have spelled out some of the awful consequences of going against society's grain. They want to dare greatly. They want to taste the fruits of values-in-action. The adolescent's world is fraught with change; its charms "are wound up," its horizons are pulsing with expectancies and actualities. His most heartfelt cry is, as Sherwood Anderson warned us long ago, "I want to know why!" The pastel, gum-drop fiction that has been wrought for him avoids both question and answer.

We might not be able to do very much very quickly about the over-innocuous quality of teen-age fiction. We need not break faith with the teen-ager by keeping him from the lifeline of prose that is there for the taking. If we accept such a commitment we take upon ourselves a living burden. We will have to teach more fervently, more honestly, more prayerfully than many of us ever have. We may have to scuttle some of the shabbily genteel lesson plans we have built around the books that have been friendly to us. Some teachers may find that they will have to begin reading all over again. (Let us face the horrible fact that some of us stop creative reading as soon as we get beyond the campus.) It is not enough to subscribe to neatly titled textbook series that are labeled "Adventures in This or That." The reading life is an adventurous life. It is open not only to the "bookish"; in fact, in a certain sense it is never open to them. The reading life is the source of much of the moral and intellectual and creative powers that insure the humanizing of man. Let us help the youngsters help themselves to it.

"The Teenage Novel: A Critique" by Vivian J. MacQuown, School Library Journal, 11:34-37, April 15, 1964. Reprinted with the permission of the publisher.

A teenage romance is a book written to fairly rigid specifications for girls between the ages of 12 and 18. The heroine should be a person of the upper middle class and she must have a problem to solve. The problem must be solved in approximately 200 attractively bound pages, in reasonably good English, with virtue triumphant.

One of the serious failings of writing to such a pattern is that the characters are cardboard and the plots contrived. Stereotyped characters and unconvincing plots may emerge as the result of unskillful writing but I suspect that, in the case of the teenage novel, they arise from the strict and narrow form. To limit one's audience to immature girls and to observe all the pious rules must surely stifle creative literary efforts. In fact, I submit that it is almost impossible to write a true work of art under the ground rules of this genre.

In the first place, there is the pitfall of language. Nothing, not even their clothing styles, is as ephemeral as the vernacular of teenagers. Before many of us realize that "square" meant anything but equilateral and equiangular, it was already square to use the word as slang. Read some of the conversations in Janet Lambert's Star Spangled Summer or Delores Lehr's The Tender Age, for example. They simply ring false. One way out of this difficulty is to write historical or period novels, as Elizabeth Speare has done so splendidly, or to write regional books like Anne Emery's Mountain Laurel.

In the teenage novel, almost without exception the young heroine will have outstanding talent in some field: music (Emery's A Dream to Touch), art (Cavanna's Going on Sixteen), (Lehr's Tender Age), weaving (Emery's Mountain Laurel) or riding (Lambert's Star Spangled Summer). She will have one or two parents who are unfailingly loving and understanding. She will have one or two boy friends, though never more and, by the end of the book, only one. She will face and solve one problem in the book, perhaps in a matter of career, but more probably one of social relationship, and by the last page will be interchangeable with the heroines of a dozen or perhaps a hundred other such books. These are not characters; they are stereotypes.

The plots of teenage novels amount to the statement of a problem and its solution, which makes them puzzles or games, rather than genuine plots. E. M. Forster, in Aspects of the Novel, says that a plot is a narrative of events which arouses not only the curiosity of the reader but his intelligence and his memory. "Characters, to be real," he says, "ought to run smoothly, but a plot ought to cause surprise." But what could be more predictable than the plot of the ordinary teenage novel?

It is only fair to say at this point that some writers have a much better record than others in this matter. Mary Stolz, for instance, writes movingly in To Tell Your Love of the heartbreak of a 17-year-old girl whose first true love abandons her for no reason that she can discover; and by the end of the book he has not come back, nor will he. In Because of Madeleine this same author describes the career of an arrogant underprivileged girl who is awarded a scholarship to an exclusive, expensive private school. No, she is never accepted as a member of the gang nor does she want to be. But she is a brilliant student and gets what she wants from life, to the bewilderment of the "establishment."

These books are exceptions in the great sea of stories where girl loses but regains boy, where she is a misfit among her companions but is finally accepted, where she fails in the preliminary talent show but wins the big one. I contend that large doses of this sort of Sunday-supplement schmaltz are unworthy of the majority of young people.

Defenders of the teenage romance, such as Anne Emery and James Summers, insist that it is unfair to derogate a whole genre, that each book should be judged on it (sic) own merits. I quite agree, but I feel certain that if these books were measured by the same standards which apply to fiction in general, there would not be so many of them on the shelves.

There are probably many who would agree with Carolyn Leopold that children are being forced to mature too rapidly, that they have not reached an emotional level to appreciate adult books. Is it not possible, however, that the mind may respond to books as the body does to all-purpose vitamins—absorb what it needs and slough off what it can't assimilate? No one would expect a 12-year-old girl to read and understand Proust, but she will never read him if her reading preparation is entirely or even primarily in the field of the teenage romance.

Some librarians who may not concur in Miss Leopold's let-them-be-young-while-they-can belief, still stock a great many of these innocuous novels because they are beset with so many self-appointed censors of the more mature books. Even though the librarian may be convinced of the value of vicarious experience, good or bad, to be gained through reading, it is usually impossible for him to convert the type of adult censor who insists on nothing but "wholesomeness" in the child's environment. Unless the librarian is prepared to engage in a crusade, the safe way out of these situations is to order some more teenage novels and leave the controversial books in the adult department.

Still another group of defenders of the junior novel are those teachers and librarians who are working with and trying to encourage slow readers, the many adolescents whose reading ability is still at an elementary level, whose interests have gone beyond the grade school texts but whose reading skill has not. This problem, it seems to me, is the best justification for the teenage book of fiction. But surely from this standpoint the books are remedial and specialized and should not make up such a large part of the fiction collection.

It is my belief that the only thing wrong with the teenage romance is its limited scope. Preoccupation with the young heroine is so single-minded that the reader has no true feeling even of the family she lives in, let alone the world. This is not a fair representation of young people. Of course they are concerned with their own immediate affairs, (Who is not?) but they are not exclusively so concerned. If the novel is supposed to be a slice of life, the teenage novel is a thin slice indeed.

What, then, should the librarian do? The answer is stated in almost every professional publication. She must know the books and know the readers! If she knows the reader she will be able to judge when to suggest a step beyond the trite junior novel, perhaps to Marguerite Bro's Sarah, Willa Cather's My Antonia or One of Ours; to the family stories of Bess Streeter Aldrich or Gladys Hasty Carroll. She will recognize the readiness for the Jalna stories or the Forsyte Saga.

I mention only domestic or home-centered adult novels, which might be considered extensions of the microcosm of the teenage book, though there is a vast realm of adventure, mystery or historical stories which may prove even more interesting to the reader who is once introduced to them. The librarian should not ban the teenage romance. Such a thought violates the creed of the profession, and indeed some of these books serve a very useful function. But she should select them on the basis of the highest possible standards and above all she should have plenty of more mature books for her young readers to grow into. As Amelia Munson says in An Ample Field, it is a librarian's duty not only to provide the books people want but also to provide those they don't know they want.

From Admiral Rickover to the neighborhood or office coffee-break, people are wondering about the value of sugar-coating every pill of knowledge. They may also doubt the worth of a whole class of literature which deals only with a very narrow segment of American youth. Most librarians would probably agree that it is all right for young people to read the junior novels but that they should move beyond them with all deliberate speed.

"Why Not the Bobbsey Twins?" by Margaret Beckman. *Ontario Library Review*, 48:148-150. Reprinted with the permission of the publisher.

It all started quite innocently, with me saying to the board member sitting next to me:

"Guess what Susan brought home from the school library today?"

"What?"

"Nancy Drew!"

For the person to whom my remark was made no explanation of my concern was necessary, because she also is a former children's librarian. But the board member across the table from us leaned over and asked, "What's the matter with Nancy Drew!"

Unobserved, the newspaper reporter began writing, and I was at the beginning of a rather horrible experience. Within a few hours of her story, a mild little account buried in the back pages of the Kitchener-Waterloo *Record*, the phone started to ring (the first call incidentally, being from the *Globe & Mail*), and it didn't stop for days. The University of Waterloo publicity director had to forget what he had planned to do the next day, and handle the people from the Toronto papers; the *Star* even sent a photographer. I was the subject of TV and radio telethons and panel shows; columnists and commentators had a field day. Within a few days mail began to arrive, until at last count there were almost 50 letters, from Cape Breton Island to Trail, British Columbia. You may be surprised to know that the majority of the writers praised my stand (if I had made one), but there were some quite vicious letters; one from a Scarborough woman who announced she was praying for my neglected daughter!

From this distance, looking back, the Bobbsey Twin affair is really quite funny, although it wasn't at the time. But I am sure, amusing as it all may have been, there are many of you wondering, as did my fellow board member, why I was concerned or annoyed at all! What is the matter with Nancy Drew! Why not the Bobbsey Twins, indeed!

No Book Ban

Let me make it quite clear, I am not advocating the banning of any books, the Vancouver Daily Times not withstanding. I am only saying the Bobbsey Twins and others like them should not be in any school library. I would react the same way if any children's school announced the showing of horror movies, or gave away comic books as prizes for perfect marks in arithmetic. It seems to me that school libraries should have the same standards as do our public libraries. Children's librarians have been saying for years that these books should not be on library shelves. What is their reason?

In the first place, it is a matter of cost. There is never enough money to buy all the new books the librarian would like to have, and so she has to select from the many titles published each year those which are to be added to the library. The children's librarian's judgment is based on an intensive study of all children's literature (both good and bad) at library school; on the reading of hundreds of children's books each year; and, most important, on the reaction of thousands of children who come in to the library to love or neglect the books she has chosen. It is the books that the children themselves love that find their way into the permanent collection, to be replaced again and again, so that each succeeding generation of children may have them to enjoy. For little children, it is Ferdinand and Curious George, Madeline and Babar; for their older brothers and sisters it could be Stuart Little or Mr. Popper, or the Black Stallion or Swallows and Amazons. All these books, and the other thousands like them, have this in common: they possess integrity and style, and some portion of the fundamental truth of life. The authors spent time and gave of themselves in the creation of these books, not giving less because they were "only" writing for children. This cannot be said of the Bobbsey Twins. Mass-produced by hired hacks, the story outlined by one writer, the dialogue sometimes filled in by another, they do not fit the criterion that we should select the best when we can't buy all. If it is the responsibility of teachers and librarians to provide the best there is for our children, then surely no public funds should be spent on this sort of trash.

The Crucial Years

The second reason is a matter of time. Despite the ardent pleas of all the experts who write newspaper columns—from the one in Winnipeg who blamed the controversy on higher education for women, to the one in Vancouver who announced that "I have rocks in my head" because I recommended Wind in the Willows (my husband's and youngest son's, "at the moment" favourite read-aloud book)—I disagree most strenuously that there is no harm done in reading the Bobbsey Twins and Nancy Drew, etc. There are only six to eight years in which a child can read, as a child, and there are so many wonderful books to be read he will never have time to read them all. To waste these few precious years reading the less than worthwhile is really a crime. Admittedly the missed books could be read when one is an adult. I read Wind in the Willows for the first time when I read it aloud to my oldest son. I enjoyed what will undoubtedly become another children's classic, The Incredible Journey, last year when the children were reading (or being read) it. But as an adult, I could not experience the wonderful delight of my six-year-old as he lived in the world of Ratty and Mole. My daughter cried tears of joy when the old terrier finished his journey and came down the path into the arms of his young master. It is only for these few short years that children, with their unique imaginations, can travel through the world of Robin Hood or Freddy the Detective. Can we knowingly deny them this opportunity?

The final reason is the effect of Bobbsey Twin reading on youthful minds. Certainly I know there are some children who are omnivorous readers, who will read, unencouraged, everything they can find and jump easily from the Hardy Boys to Treasure Island. But this is where the newspaper experts make their mistake. They assume all children can or will do this, because some of the few children with whom they are familiar have been able to. I would like them to work for just a few weeks as a children's librarian and listen to the parents who come in to the library wringing their hands because Johnny hasn't read anything since he finished the Hardy Boys. Johnny is typical of the many many more children who are not omnivorous readers, who never make the transition from one kind of reading to another. The extent of their reading is the mind-stultifying series books. A child's mind needs to stretch and grow, and it can reach for far horizons if it is challenged. But if it is not challenged, it will follow the path of least resistance, and memories of childhood reading will be something mildly pleasant, perhaps, but unstimulating. The many high school students who have to be cajoled and even forced into reading their six compulsory supplementary reading books, are examples of children for whom childhood reading was not a stimulating or challenging experience. The disgraceful statistics which show that North American adults read far fewer books than do their English, Swedish, and Russian counterparts, can, I suggest, be traced to the same cause.

But this need not be! Ask any children's librarian and she can give you dozens of examples of children who weren't interested in reading—who had had the "Bobbsey Twin bit" and were (yes, I still use the word) bored; or who had had difficulty learning to read, at school, and for whom reading and pleasure were not associated.

With skill, and sometimes luck, the librarian was able to introduce this child to just the right book for him, at the right time. The next week she had another. . . and that child is off in a new world, a confirmed reader for life. Having watched this happen many times in the children's library, and then, much more personally, in my own family, I can only say it has been one of my greatest satisfactions.

But, judging from the letters I have received from children asking "What else is there for me to read?" we have not been doing our job well enough. If there are children in this province who do not have access to a good children's library, then it is our responsibility as trustees to do our utmost to ensure that no child be denied this opportunity. And since there are obviously parents and teachers and newspaper columnists who are not aware of the wonderful books the children could be reading, books no child should miss, then I also suggest that the librarians in this province have not been doing their job either. After all, children's librarians have been undermining the Bobbsey Twins for 25 years, but they haven't been too successful. Of course they, no more than I, suggest the books be banned: if Aunt Harriet insists on giving Junior a Hardy Boy every Christmas, no one will complain. But the work librarians are doing must be understand, and explained, and publicized. Everyone should be made aware of the joyful experience of introducing a little boy who hadn't read anything but Dick and Jane to the Twenty-one Balloons, and having him come in to the library the next week with stars in his eyes and ask for another book "just like that one." And if you have a qualified children's librarian in your library, you as trustees should support her. Please don't, as one trustee did this winter, disagree publicly with your librarian's position in a professional matter. When asked her opinion about the Bobbsey Twins, this trustee, knowing (at least let's hope she knew) that the library on whose board she serves does not have this type of book, based her reply on her experience with her own children, and said "The important thing is to induce a child to take an interest in reading," whether it's the Bobbsey Twins or not. The librarian, basing her opinion on work with thousands of children, gave a diametrically opposing view. The resulting article is most unfortunate.

But there it is! If we feel that public funds can be spent on the mediocre rather than on books of lasting value; if we feel we can afford to waste any child's time and deprive him of his heritage of the world's children's literature; and if we feel that it isn't important that he be so excited by his adventures in reading that he carry the memories with him into adult life, then the Bobbsey Twins and Nancy Drew don't matter. But if we are librarians and trustees who sincerely believe that reading is vital, we will remember that a child wants only the best until we, as adults, teach him to accept mediocrity. We will place before him the world of books, and guide his footsteps through the realms of fantasy and adventure, history and science. We will realize that this isn't the easiest way, but we will know that the rewards are very very great.

"Comic Books: A Teacher's Analysis" by Dwight L. Burton, Elementary School Journal, 56:73-75, October, 1955. University of Chicago Press. Copyright 1966 by The University of Chicago.

Comic books are back in the headlines. Much of the current public furor is traceable to a book by Frederic Wertham,[1] a New York psychiatrist, who contends that comic books promote, among other undesirable outcomes, illiteracy, unwholesome states of mind, and delinquent behavior. The NEA Journal, in its November, 1954, issue,[2] designates Dr. Wertham's book as "the most important book of 1954" and admonishes local education associations and parent-teacher associations to "see that it is widely read and that the community takes steps to protect children from the menace it describes."

Children and adults now buy more than one billion comic books each year, and, with deadly regularity, studies of children's voluntary reading show comics heading the list, particularly among children in Grades IV-VIII. Public and professional concern over this interest in the comics is not new. A check of the Readers' Guide to Periodical Literature shows that since 1945 more than 250 essays and articles on comics have appeared in American periodicals, including such journals as the Saturday Review, the Atlantic Monthly, the New Yorker, and Phi Beta Kappa's American Scholar.

Teachers long have shared in the general concern over the wide reading of comic books and their impact upon children's minds. Several years ago the National Council of Teachers of English published an article entitled "Substitutes for the Comics."[3] As professional people, teachers should make sure that lay groups are familiar with the materials mentioned and with others, such as the December, 1941, issue of the Journal of Experimental Education and the December, 1949, issue of the Journal of Educational Sociology, which present research relative to comics. The findings of research, in the main, fail to support the conclusions of Dr. Wertham. Without acting as an apologist for objectionable comic books, the teacher has an obligation to make research findings available to groups discussing the matter.

Basic Appeals of the Comic Books

Elementary-school teachers interested in developing reading interests and tastes of children have an additional stake in understanding children's zest for the comic books. Might not the comics be a foot in the door to success in guiding children to more profitable reading experiences? Carr has advised:

> If the teacher or parent is concerned about a child's growth in appreciation of "good" books, let him start with the present level of the child and initiate him into books that attract him with the same qualities of adventure, excitement, and humor that he is meeting in comic books. [4]

What, then, are the basic appeals of the comic books?

Probably the most obvious appeal of the comics lies in the ease with which they can be read and understood. The vocabulary of the comics is not particularly easy; one study estimates the difficulty level at fifth to seventh grade.[5] This is unimportant, however, for the actual text need not be read at all. Looking at the pictures and reading a word here and there are enough to get the story. Superior readers may read as many comics as inferior readers, but the poor reader especially may be attracted to the comics if the required or recommended reading in class is continually beyond him.

Certainly another of the basic attractions of the comic books is that they appeal immediately to more senses than does straight reading. Little imaginative effort is necessary to read them. The reader need not conjure up his own images. The characters, complete with bulging biceps and golden tresses or patently evil visages, and the situations are there already in bright colors. The comics are therefore a haven for the lazy or sluggish imagination.

Then, too, the content of the comic magazines is highly compatible with the nature of children in preadolescence or early adolescence, the period when comics are at their peak of popularity.

Although the content is highly varied, common to all the comic magazines are the magic ingredients of action, suspense, mystery, and adventure—adding up to "punch" in the mind of the young reader. The frequent stress on the fantastic or the bizarre is in line with the wild flights to which the imagination is inclined in late childhood and early adolescence. The main characters in the comics tend to be either supermen, who represent a kind of ideal fulfilment, or simpletons to whom one can feel superior. Says Al Capp, creator of Li'l Abner, "When Yokum speaks, he speaks for millions of morons."

The appeal of the comics is rooted, too, in the fact that their picture of life and the assumptions underlying it are naturally acceptable to the immature mind of the reader. This is true of all "trash" literature and of many motion pictures and radio and television programs. That life is an exciting physical adventure is one assumption of the immature mind. Another is that people are either all good or all bad, with no intermediate degrees, and that one can tell the difference usually by physical appearance alone. One just knows that clean-cut Roy Rogers is a "good guy" while his unshaven adversaries are crooks. The outlaws in "Dick Tracy" and "Batman" usually have revolting physical characteristics and mannerisms. Another assumption undergirding comic-book experience is that romantic love and money lie at the heart of the problems of life. Still another is that the end justifies the means: it matters not that Superman kills a few people here and there and destroys countless dollars' worth of property, for he is on the side of right. In the comics, people in authority—policemen, mayors, senators, teachers, parents, corporation heads—tend to be stupid, pompous, or sadistic, and inevitably they are humiliated. How appealing is this to the younster who is so much under the thumb of adult authority! The rebellion against authority, whether of the Bugs Bunny or Li'l Abner variety, is a very real appeal.

Finally, of course, the success of the comic books is aided by their low cost and their availability.

Transition Books

Once the teacher has made an analysis of the basic appeals of the comic books, he is in a position to construct a ladder out of the aesthetic wasteland which they represent by steering pupils to selections which contain the same basic appeals yet represent a step upward toward a more mature and wholesome reading experience. What qualities should these "transition" materials have?

1. They must be easy to read, appropriate to the reader's level. Difficulty in recognizing more than one in one hundred words will quickly kill the pleasure element in reading. Though the reading level is low, the selection still may be aesthetically satisfying, as writers like Eleanor Estes, Doris Gates, and Stephen Meader have demonstrated.

2. It is also most important that transition materials reflect experience close to that of the reader. Identification with characters and situations is a keystone of appreciation in reading and, for most pupils at the early adolescent and late childhood level, this identification must be literal. Only mature readers develop the ability to make abstract identifications with characters and situations. It is psychologically impossible for the pupil to jump from the comics to a pleasurable reading of Evangeline. Preferably, characters in these transition selections should be of about the age of the reader, and their experiences should be of the familiar or the exciting kind with which the reader wants to identify.

3. Transition books must avoid the gross distortion of experience that is characteristic of the comics. Yet the experience represented should be simple, since life for most young readers is relatively uncomplicated. Action still will occur mostly on the physical plane, but the plots should avoid the wild coincidence and improbability of many of the comics. True, the young protagonists often will do surpassing things in a world curiously detached from adult control, but perhaps we can accept this at this stage. Traumatic experiences involving excessive violence and the sordid should be avoided.

4. These materials must have the magic ingredients of "punch"; action, suspense, peril are the watchwords. Pupils should

not get the idea that the books on the teacher's recommended list are likely to be dull.

5. Finally, transition materials must be made as available as possible. Classroom libraries, book exhibits and bazaars, bulletin-board displays of book jackets will help. Parent-teacher associations and other lay groups interested in combating the comic-book "menace" might concern themselves with making other reading materials more plentiful and available for children.

What are some selections and types of selections which fit these characteristics? The area of folklore offers rich possibilities as an antidote for comics. Each region of the country has its folklore, which can be appreciated at various levels of awareness but which has much in common with the comics: the lusty, sometimes slapstick, humor; the action; the quality of the unusual and amazing; the superheroes. Yet all of this is of a much richer, more wholesome, and more artful fabric than the comics display.

Many of the selections in such series as the Bobbs-Merrill (Indianapolis) "Childhood of Famous Americans, " with its simple biographies of Davy Crockett, Narcissa Whitman, and others, fit this transition category for third- and fourth-graders. So might the "Landmark" and "World Landmark" books of Random House (New York), with the stories of General Custer, the FBI, and the Battle of Britain, among many others, serve this purpose with fifth- and sixth-graders. The "American Adventure" series of Wheeler Publishing Company (Chicago) and the "Real People" series of Row, Peterson and Company (Evanston, Illinois) are in the same category. These books are useful as supplementary materials in the social-studies field, and some of the selections provide literary experiences in their own right. A few examples of writers whose books fill the transition need in Grades VII and VIII are Jim Kjelgaard, Montgomery Atwater, Doris Gates, Shannon Garst, Stephen Meader, Kenneth Gilbert, and Howard Pease.

A healthful viewpoint toward comic books is summarized in a statement of the faculty of the Whittier Elementary School in Minneapolis:

Those of us who hope to guide children's tastes and especially their reading interests must certainly take note that the comics are a form of reading each child takes to without coaxing. . . .

With adult guidance the comics may serve as a bridge to the reading of more lasting books. We must help our children discover good books that are exciting too and teach them to discriminate among comic books; then we may safely accept our children's comic reading for what it is—a stage in their growth—provided we also help them toward wider horizons of interest and appreciation.[6]

Notes

1. Frederick Wertham, Seduction of the Innocent. New York: Rinehart & Co., Inc., 1954.

2. Joy Elmer Morgan, "Seduction of the Innocent," NEA Journal, XLIII (November, 1954), p. 473.

3. Constance Carr, "Substitutes for the Comics," Elementary English, XXVIII (April and May, 1951), p. 194-200, 276-85. These articles were reprinted in a pamphlet, which is now out of print while undergoing revision.

4. Ibid., p. 194.

5. Robert L. Thorndike, "Words and the Comics," Journal of Experimental Education, X (December, 1941), p. 110-13.

6. Guide to the Teaching of Reading in the Elementary School, p. 130. Minneapolis, Minnesota: Division of Elementary Education, Public Schools, 1950.

Part Five. Giving A Book Talk

"Book Talks" by Amelia H. Munson. From An Ample Field, by Amelia H. Munson. Chicago, American Library Association, 1950. Reprinted with the permission of the American Library Association.

Library work begins and ends with the individual. It welcomes group work but only as a way of reaching additional individuals. It responds to group requests but realizes that its response must be adapted to the varying capacities of the individual members. One of the most satisfactory means for reaching young people and interesting them in books is through the medium of book talks given before all kinds of groups.

Foreknowledge of the group is desirable: age, sex, interests, current employment, intellectual attainment. The problem then becomes one of finding books that will reflect and hold their interest (and about which you yourself can be enthusiastic) and working out the best manner of presenting these books within strict time limits. They need not be new books, as Christopher Morley once pointed out. Writing in the Saturday Review of Literature, he had occasion to refer to his visit at the Crime Detection Laboratory at Northwestern University.

> There they have invented a way of reviving the most faded or perished inkscript. Unless the actual fabric of the paper has been destroyed, the ink leaves iron residues; and by blowing a gas upon an apparently blank sheet these particles of iron can be corroded so that the former writing leaps to sight, now rusted brilliant red. It struck me that here was a shiny parable for teachers of literature. Their topic is often ancient books and papers, from which the childish pupil might suppose all life had withered. But if the teacher has the right kind of gas on spout, handwriting as old as Chaucer can burn again more vivid than tonight's tabloid. Presuming that it had, to begin with, the authentic mettle.

It is often wise to inject a few remarks about old favorites since it will add the reasurance of familiarity. They need not be primarily books of difficulty that need introduction. There is need for "bait" with a good many young people, and the approving mention of books that simply walk off from your shelves without even a friendly and understanding attitude toward young people's reading.

Some librarians are tempted, looking at their shelves and seeing books that continue to stay there unread, simply to load up with an armful and go before a group to talk about them. That may be profitable, if you know your group very well, if you meet with them often, and if they have come to trust your judgment. But the opportunity that is afforded by book talks is not for the clearing of your shelves but the uncovering of individual interests and tastes and needs.

It is probably wise to start with the local, the immediate, the contemporary, to dispel at once any notion that a person working with books has no idea of what is happening in the world around him. Not only news and current happenings but radio programs and movies can supply you with opening sentences. From there move swiftly into the connecting book, by incident or character or conversation, and tell what you have come to tell with gusto and dispatch, savoring your recollection of the book as you go along and presenting it so that its special appeal, the thing that sets it apart from all other books, is apparent. Too many people, charmed by a fine piece of biographical writing, fall into the error, when facing a group and talking about it, of giving the bare facts of the subject's life and a summary of his accomplishments. They would be horrified if you told them so, for the book is clear in their minds and their remembrance of it pleases them even as they talk, but they fail to convey any part of the book's charm. They might have been reading an article in the encyclopedia for all their auditors can make of it. The whole distinction of the book is lost.

The book talk falls into place between storytelling and book reviewing, partakes of both and is unlike either. At its best, it sounds informal and spontaneous and in such harmony with the group addressed that it seems like conversation or discussion rather than a monologue. Back of this seeming spontaneity, however, lie careful preparation and organization of material.

Think of the group you are to address, visualize them in your mind's eye, place yourself among them, at one with them in their occupations and surroundings, and cock an ear toward the speaker who is just taking up his position in front of the group. What do you want to hear? How do you wish to be addressed? How long can you sit still and listen? Now, with that anticipation, consider your resources. You have the whole world of books to choose from. Choose wisely, then, the book you will present and refresh your recollection of it; then you must prove, simply by your presentation, that it is worth reading. It will do no good to say that it is exciting or thrilling: your youthful audience sits unmoved; obviously it is exciting or why would anyone want to talk about it? They wait for evidence of the kind of excitement they will find: the story must show it. Keep your rendition of it moving along; don't let the narrative bog down in details; don't clutter the listener's mind with too many characters to keep track of; keep your facts well in hand and well reined in and drive on to a high moment, either of drama or suspense. Leave it there, and, after enough of a pause to loose your audience from the spell of the book, turn to another, one that follows naturally, alike in some way or distinguished for its utter dissimilarity.

Watch your listeners as you talk—all of them—and see to it that you have something of interest for everyone, that before you finish, all of them will have heard something to remember. The friendliness of your manner, the sincerity of your approach, the understanding of your presentation, and the evidence of your respect for their opinion should make it easy for them to seek you out afterward and ask questions.

Naturally you'll make yourself heard by everyone and not confine your remarks to the first row or two, but you will capture their attention, not demand it. You might remember, too, that young people study Oral English and are quick to note carelessness in diction, sentence construction, posture, and all the rest. Is it necessary to add that of course you will not use notes and that the books you talk about will be in your hands as you speak and available from your library later on?

If you are talking about novels or biography, make the characters live as they live on the pages. Let them walk out of the books and into the lives of your listeners. Sketch them vividly in a few words so that they are recognizable, and give concrete examples of their actions, not some abstract generalizations as to their line of conduct. Even though your zeal to make your auditors want to read the book for themselves tempts you to over-ornamentation, avoid it sternly. Better lose readers than have readers disappointed through your excess of enthusiasm.

Sometimes your desire to "be faithful to the book" will persuade you that reading aloud from it will be far more effective than relating the story in your own words. "The author can say it much better." Very likely, else you yourself would be an author, but right now it is your job to talk. You have established a rapport with your group; they are giving you their attention and enjoying it; things are moving along rapidly and well. Don't jeopardize that relationship; go on telling in your own words (heightened perhaps by phrases remembered from the author's own recital) and to the very best of your ability "what happened next."

The only legitimate time for you to read to a group is when you are presenting material in which the author's style is the important thing and can be communicated in no other way: Poetry, some essays, fine writing in general. Even then you would do well to quote rather than to read or know the book so well that you are not bound to it—your eyes can still rove over the group and take cognizance of their enjoyment, be watchful for signs of disinterest.

If you are presenting factual material or technical books, be very sure of your terms, and be able to bandy them about masterfully. Sharpen your descriptions. Strive always for the concrete instance, the definite fact.

And throw in something definitely beyond their expectations even if it occasionally goes over their heads. Sometimes a casual phrase, an interpolated reference to advanced material may be the one thing to catch a reader's attention and start him off on a quest of his own. Pay them the compliment of assuming that they are willing and eager to stretch their minds even when all evidence would seem to point to the contrary.

Know beforehand what your allotment of time is to be and keep well within it. Plan your talk thoroughly in a kind of outline or within a frame, force yourself to practice it aloud with your watch in your hand and cut drastically where necessary. If you retain too much or are unwilling to plan and, therefore, improvise and expand as you go along, you will find yourself hurrying your speech and talking briskly with no room for the little play of stress and drawl and pause that can be so effective and that make for informality. Your listeners are not going to be at ease unless you are at ease; so be sure of your material. Otherwise you may find yourself looking at your watch and commenting on the shabbily few minutes you have, thus transferring everyone's attention from the matter at hand to an anxiety lest you fail to stop in time. Be sure you do that—stop in time—before interest wanes. You may be asked to come again.

Index

"The Adolescent in American Literature," 59-68
Adventure stories, 49-58
All About the Planets, 102, 107-108
All About the Stars, 103, 109
All-American, 165, 181
Alm, Richard S., 150-161
An American Tragedy, 25, 30
Amos Fortune: Free Man, 112
An Ample Field, 198
And Both Were Young, 166
And Ride Forth Singing, 76
Andersonville, 119
Animal stories, 160-161, 190-191
Anne Frank: The Diary of a Young Girl, 71
Annixter, Paul, 54, 56, 161, 163-164
Another Country, 28
Ant Men, 175
Anthem, 32
Asimov, Isaac, 105
Aspects of the Novel, 196
"Astronomy Books for Children", 99-109
Atwater, Montgomery, 53

Baker, Augusta, 110
Baker, Nina Brown, 87
Baker, Rachel, 83
Baker, Robert H., 104-105
Baldwin, James, 28-29
The Barred Road, 112, 181
Because of Madeline, 179-180, 196
Beckman, Margaret, 199
Behind the Ranges, 54
Benét, Stephen Vincent, 143
The Big Inning, 182-183
Binder, Otto, 105-106
"Biographies for Teen-Agers", 79-89
Biography, 37-38, 79-89, 111-112, 208

Black Boy, 61, 68
The Black Tiger, 176
Blanton, Miriam, 112, 181
Blau, Lois, 45-48
Bobbsey Twins, 199-203
A Book of Planets for You, 106
"Book Talks", 211-215
"Books About Negroes for Children", 110-114
Booth, W. C., 117-132
Bound for Singapore, 56
Bowen, Robert, 182-183
Boylston, Helen, 152
Brandwein, Paul F., 104
Branley, F. M., 100, 101-103, 106
Brecht, Bertolt, 31-32
Breck, Vivian, 54
Brighter Than a Thousand Suns, 30
Bro, Marguerite Harmon, 158
Buck, Pearl, 73, 76-77
Bugbee, Emma, 152
Bulman, Learned T., 79-89
Burton, Dwight, 116, 156, 162-171, 204-209

Cady, Edwin H., 7-15
The Caine Mutiny, 74
Call It Courage, 55
Camus, Albert, 31
Canady, John, 28
A Candle for St. Jude, 158
Candy Kane, 151-152
A Cap for Mary Ellis, 112
Capp, Al, 206
Career stories, 112, 152-153, 190
Carlsen, G. Robert, 16-25, 49-58, 176
Carpenter, Frederic, 59-68
Carry On, Mr. Bowditch, 85-86
Cash, W. J., 29
Catcher In the Rye, 21, 36, 46, 60-63, 120-123, 126-131
Cather, Willa, 33, 76
Cavanna, Betty, 70, 155-156, 164-165

217

Censorship, 47-48, 115, 117-149
"Censorship and High School Libraries", 133-135
"Censorship and Sex in Contemporary Society", 146
"Censorship and the Values of Fiction", 117-132
Chaim Weizman, 83
A Chance to Belong, 182
Chemmeen, 30
Chequer Board, 76
The City Boy, 67
A City for Lincoln, 165-166
Clarence Darrow, 84-85
Comets, 109
Comic books, 115-116, 141-144, 204-209
"Comic Books: A Teacher's Analysis", 204-209
Compass Rose, 74
The Cool World, 30
Cosmic View, 107
Cowboy Boots, 55
Cox, William, 183
Cress Delahanty, 59, 65-67
Crime and Punishment, 22
The Cruel Sea, 74-75
Cummings, E. E., 123-124
A Cup of Courage, 178
Cyclone in Calico, 87

Daly, Maureen, 70-73, 156, 162-163
The Dark Adventure, 57
Darkness at Noon, 30
Das Kapital, 141-142
"Death in the Country", 143
Death of a Salesman, 28
Decker, Duane, 183
De Leeuw, Adele, 112, 181
The Deputy, 30
Desmond, Alice, 83-84
Dickens, Charles, 74
A Dipper Full of Stars, 108
Divided Heart, 179
Douglas, Gilbert, 113
Dreiser, Theodore, 18, 30
Du Jardin, Rosemary, 177
Du Soe, Robert, 53

Earth and High Heaven, 76
East Wind, West Wind, 77

Eaton, Jeannette, 81-82
Edmonds, Walter D., 76
Edwards, Margaret, 26-34, 69-77, 156, 172-185
Ellison, Ralph, 67-68
Emery, Anne, 154-155, 177
Epstein, Samuel, 86
Escape from Freedom, 30
Esslin, Martin, 31
Exploring Mars, 106
Exploring the Planets, 106-107
Exploring the Universe, 99

Farmer in the Sky, 57
Fast, Howard, 21
Felsen, Henry Gregor, 36, 155-156, 175, 180
Fenton, C. L., 106
Find the Constellations, 108
"Finding the Right Poem", 90-98
The Fire Balloon, 168-169
The Fire Next Time, 29
First Book of Astronomy, 101
First on a Rope, 54
Five Against the Odds, 183
Five Were Chosen, 183
Folklore, 94-95, 208
Follett, Wilson, 186
"For Esmé—With Love and Squalor", 63
"For Everything There is a Season", 16-25
Forbes, Esther, 160
Forester, C. S., 167, 169-170
Forster, E. M., 196
Fourth Out, 183
Franny and Zooey, 28
Freedman, Benedict and Nancy, 73
Freeman, Mae and Ira, 102, 106
Frick, C. H., 183
The Friendly Persuasion, 66-67
Fromm, Erich, 30
Fun With Astronomy, 102-103, 106

Gallant, Roy A., 99, 106-107
Gamow, George, 107
Gannon, Richard D., 133-135
Garst, Shannon, 55, 81-82
Gault, William C., 176, 183
Gerson, Corinne, 182

218

A Girl Can Dream, 155-156
Girl Trouble, 178
"The Glitter and the Gold", 150-161
Go Tell it on the Mountain, 28
Godden, Rumer, 76, 158
Going on Sixteen, 70, 155, 164-165
Going Steady, 155, 177
Golden Book of Astronomy, 102, 109
Golden Footlights, 86
Goodbye, My Lady, 161
Goodin, Peggy, 182
The Gown of Glory, 72-73
Graham, Frank, 88
Graham, Lorenz, 113
Graham, Shirley, 85
Gray, James, 168
The Great Houdini, 86
Grey, Vivian, 101, 107
Gurko, Leo, 86

Hank Winton series, 53
Hanna, Geneva, 35-40
Hard to Tackle, 113
The Hard Way, 184
Harkins, Phillip, 176
Harlow, Alvin, 83
Hart, Hazel, 41-44
Hawkins, G. S., 104
The Heart is a Lonely Hunter, 61, 64-65
Heart of Danger, 56
Heinlein, Robert, 54-55, 57
Hersey, John, 29
Herzberg, Max, 94
Hie to the Hunters, 159
High Trail, 54
Historical fiction, 75, 111-112
Hit and Run, 183
Hochhuth, Rolf, 30
Hold Fast to Your Dreams, 112, 181
Hot Rod, 155, 175-176
Hot rod stories, 175-176
"How Do I Love Thee?" 69-77
Huckleberry Finn, 60, 62-63, 124, 126, 132
Hull Down for Action, 53-54

I Capture the Castle, 74
In a Mirror, 179

The Incredible Journey, 201
Infield Spark, 183
Introducing the Constellations, 105
Introduction to Astronomy, 104
Invisible Man, 68

Jackson, Phyllis W., 86
Jacobs, Emma, 182
Jane Eyre, 72, 74
Jennings, Frank G., 174, 186
Johnny Tremain, 160
Joseph Pulitzer, 84
Joy in the Morning, 23
Joyce, James, 32
Julie's Heritage, 112, 181-182
Jungk, Robert, 30
Junior Miss, 71
Junior novel, 115, 150-198
"The Junior Novels and How They Grew", 185

Kafka, Franz, 22
Kees, Boeke, 107
Keystone Kid, 181
King, Martin Luther, 29
The Kingdom of the Sun, 105
Knowles, John, 21
Koestler, Arthur, 30
Komroff, Manuel, 84

Lambert, Janet, 151-152, 195
Lamson, Mary V., 90-98
Lance of Kanana, 49-51
Lane, Rose Wilder, 72
La Paz, Lincoln and Jean, 107
Latham, Jean Lee, 85-86
Lathrop, West, 53
Lauber, Patricia, 102, 107-108
Lavine, Sigmund, 87
The Legacy, 76
Lehr, Delores, 195
L'Engle, Madeleine, 166-167
Leopard, Carolyn, 197
"Let 'Em Read Trash", 139-149
Let the Hurricane Roar, 72
"Let the Lower Lights Be Burning", 172-185
Level 7, 30
Levinger, Elma, 87
Lewiton, Mina, 178-179
Like a Sister, 182
"Literature for Adolescents — Pap or Protein?" 174, 186-194
Look Homeward, Angel, 68

Lord Hornblower, 169
Lou Gehrig, 88
Love Poems of Six Centuries, 75
The Loved One, 22
Lucy Gayheart, 33

McCullers, Carson, 61, 63
Macken, Walter, 75
MacQuown, Vivian, 195-198
MacRae, Donald and Elizabeth, 99-109
Mainstreams of Modern Art, 28
Malamud, Bernard, 32
A Man for Marcy, 177
The Many Loves of Dobie Gillis, 75
Markandaya, Kamala, 30
Marshall, Catherine, 112, 180-181
Marx, Karl, 141
Mary Ellis, Student Nurse, 112
Maugham, W. Somerset, 21
Maxwell, William, 159
May, Julian, 108
Mead, Margaret, 146
Meader, Stephen, 54, 56
Means, Florence, 112
Member of the Wedding, 64
Metamorphosis, 22
Miller, Arthur, 28
Miller, Warren, 30
The Mind of the South, 29
Minority problems, 28-30, 37-38, 47, 68, 110-113, 181-182
Mr. Fullback, 183
Mr. Quarterback, 183
Monsarrat, Nicholas, 74
Mood, Robert G., 139-149
The Moon, 107
The Moon, Earth's Natural Satellite, 106
The Moon, Our Neighboring World, 105
The Moon Seems to Change, 100-101
Moore, Ruth, 167-168
Morley, Christopher, 211
Mother Courage, 32
Mountain Tamer, 54-55
Mrs. Mike, 73-74
Munson, Amelia, 198, 211-215
My Antonia, 33
My Friend Flicka, 73

Mystery stories, 191
Mythology, 94
Myths and Their Meaning, 94

Nancy Drew, 199-203
The Natural, 32
Nectar in a Sieve, 30
"Needed: More Literature Reading", 41-44
Neely, Henry M., 108
Nelson, Jack, 131
Neurath, Marie, 108
New Dreams for Old, 113
Newell, Hope, 112
The Nine Brides and Granny Hite, 75
Nine Planets, 101-103
Noble, Iris, 84-85
Nolan, Jeanette, 81
Norris, Hoke, 136-138
North, Eric, 175
Northern Trail Adventure, 53
"The Novel for the Adolescent", 162-171
"The Novel in the High School Library", 45-48
The Nun's Story, 22

O'Connor, Patrick, 176
Of Human Bondage, 21, 28
Of Mice and Men, 65
Of Time and the River, 170
O'Hara, John, 73
Olson, Gene, 180
On Stage, Mr. Jefferson, 86
Open Season, 178

Page, Lou Williams, 108
Patterson, Emma L., 185
Pease, Howard, 56-57
Peggy Covers the News, 152
Penrod, 60
Person, Tom, 113
Peyton Place, 131
The Plague, 31
Planet: Other Worlds of our Solar System, 105-106
Poetry, 90-98, 112
Pont, Clarice, 179
Portrait of the Artist as a Young Man, 32
Pray Love, Remember, 179
Prejudice, books on, 47, 76, 181-182

Prester, John, 49-51, 55
Pride and Prejudice, 74
Prom Trouble, 178
"Promoting Adolescent Growth Through Reading", 35-40

Quality, 76
The Quest of Galileo, 108

Rain on the Wind, 75-76
Rand, Ayn, 32
Rawlings, Marjorie K., 160
The Razor's Edge, 21
Reach for a Star, 112
Reading guidance, 38-39
Reading Ladders for Human Relations, 45-46
Ready or Not, 179
The Red Car, 176
The Red Pony, 68
Reed, Maxwell, 104
Rey, H. A., 108
Rich, Louise, 56
Ripley, Elizabeth, 88-89
Rise and Fall of the Third Reich, 30
Road Race, 176
Roberts, Gene, Jr., 132
Robinson Crusoe, 57
"The Role of Literature for Young People Today", 7-15
Rolling Stones, 57-58
The Rolling Years, 72, 77
Rollins, Charlemae, 110-114
Romantic stories, 69-77, 191
Romeo and Juliet, 129
Rudaux, Lucien, 108

St. Exupery, Antoine, 28
Salinger, J. D., 46, 61-63
Sally on the Fence, 179
Sarah, 158-159
Schneider, Herman and Nina, 102, 108
Science fiction, 54-55, 175
The Sea Gulls Woke Me, 70-71, 179
Seduction of the Innocent, 116, 141
Senior Year, 154
A Separate Peace, 21
Series books, 115, 186-187, 191, 199-203

Seventeen, 67, 163
Seventeenth Summer, 70, 156-157, 162-163
Shepherd, Walter, 109
Shirer, William, 30
Shooting Star, 109
Show Me The World of Astronomy, 108
Shute, Nevil, 73, 76
Shulman, Max, 75
Sky and Forest, 170
The Small Rain, 166-167
Smith, Betty, 23
Smith, Dodie, 74
Sorority Girl, 155
South Town, 113
Space, 101
Space in your Future, 108-109
Space Nomads, 107
Sperry, Armstrong, 53-55
Spice and the Devil's Cave, 49
Splendor in the Sky, 104
Sports stories, 113, 180-184
Stanford, Don, 176
Stapp, Arthur, 54-55
Star-Spangled Summer, 152, 195
Stars, 109
The Stars By Clock and Fist, 108
Stars for Sam, 104
Start of the Trail, 56
The Steadfast Heart, 153
Steinbeck, John, 29, 65, 68
Stinetorf, Louise A., 76
Stolz, Mary, 70-71, 157-158, 179, 196
The Stranger, 31
Street, James, 161
Street Rod, 36, 155-156, 176
Stride Toward Freedom, 29
Stuart, Jesse, 159
The Students' Right to Read, 132
Sue Barton, Neighborhood Nurse, 152
Summers, James L., 177-178
Sumner, Cid R., 76
The Sun, 109
Swiftwater, 54, 56, 163-164

Take Care of My Little Girl, 182
A Tale of Two Cities, 74
The Tall One, 180
Tarkington, Booth, 60, 67, 163
Tea and Sympathy, 68

"The Teenage Novel: A Critique", 195-198
Tellander, Marian, 101, 109
The Tender Age, 195
The Theatre of the Absurd, 31
Thompson, Mary Wolfe, 153
Three Without Fear, 53
Thunder Road, 176
"A Time and Season for the Better Reader", 26-34
"To Sail Beyond the Sunset", 49-58, 176
To Tell Your Love, 70, 157-158, 179, 196
Tom Paine, Freedom's Apostle, 86
Tom Sawyer, 60, 145
Tourney Team, 183
Trap Lines North, 56-57
Travels With Charley, 29
Treasure Island, 49-51, 53, 55
Tunis, John R., 165-166, 181-182
Turnbull, Agnes, 72-73
Twain, Mark, 59-60
Two and the Town, 156, 180
"Two Kinds of Censorship", 136-138

Ullman, James R., 76
Ulysses, 73
The Universe, 109
Untermeyer, Louis, 96
Unwilling Heart, 180

Vance, Marguerite, 81-82, 84
Von Ryan's Express, 22

Waiting for Godot, 31
Walk Like a Mortal, 159-160, 167-168

Walker, Mildred 73, 158
Wandering Minstrels We, 87
War stories, 47
Waugh, Evelyn, 22
We Build Together, 110-111
Wedding Journey, 76
Weeks, Jack, 184
Wertham, Frederic, 116, 141, 204
West, Jessamyn, 59-61, 65-67
When the Stars Come Out, 105
White, Andrew T., 103, 109
White Witch Doctor, 76
Whitman, Walt, 73
"Why Not the Bobbsey Twins?" 199-203
Wickenden, Don, 159-160, 167-168
Williams, Beryl, 86
Wilson, Neill, 75
Wimmer, Helmut, 101
Wind in the Willows, 201
Wind, Sand and Stars, 28
Winter Wheat, 73, 158
Wolfe, Thomas, 33, 46-47, 68, 167, 170
Wonders of the Universe, 108
World Series, 166
Worlds in the Sky, 106
Wouk, Herman, 67
Wright, Richard, 61, 67-68
Wuthering Heights, 74
Wyler, Rose, 102, 109

Yates, Elizabeth, 112
Yea! Wildcats! 165
The Yearling, 160-161
You Among the Stars, 102, 108
You Can't Go Home Again, 170

Zim, Herbert S., 109